MT. ST. HELENA

HWY. 29

CHATEAU MONTELENA

STERLING VINEYARDS

CUVAISON

Silverado Trail

BURGESS CELLARS

Pope Valley Winery

CHARLES KRUG WINERY

BERINGER'S WINERY

SUTTER HOME WINERY

LOUIS MARTINI WINERY

HEITZ CELLARS

CALISTOGA

Tubbs Lane

HWY. 128

Petrified Forest Rd.

DIAMOND CREEK VINEYARDS

STONE GATE WINERY

Dunaweal

Larkmead Ln.

Napa River

HANNS KORNELL CHAMPAGNE CELLARS

FREEMARK ABBEY WINERY

Lodi Lane

Deer Park Rd.

HWY. 29

SCHRAMSBERG VINEYARDS

STONY HILL WINERY

SPRING MOUNTAIN VINEYARDS

CHRISTIAN BROTHERS

ST. HELENA

Spring Mt. Rd.

YVERDON WINERY

CHATEAU CHEVALIER

LYNCREST VINEYARDS

Joseph Phelps Vineyards
Tonichelini Winery
Cayous Vineyards
Chappellet Vineyards
*Stags Leap Winery
*Stag's Leap Winecellar
*Clos Duval
Hwy. 12

Silverado Trail

Napa River

Zinfandel Lane
Souverain Cellars
Rutherford Rd.
Robert Mondavi Winery
Oakville Vineyards
Yountville Cross
NAPA

RUTHERFORD

Hwy. 29

OAKVILLE

YOUNTVILLE

Franciscan Vineyards
Beaulieu Vineyards
Inglenook Vineyards

Oakville Cross

Mayacamas Winery
*Veedercrest Vineyards
*Mt. Veeder Vineyards
Redwood Rd.
Christian Brothers Mont La Salle

*Carneros Creek Winery

Los Carneros

Sonoma Hwy.

N
E
W
S

NAPA VALLEY

CALIFORNIA WINERIES

VOLUME ONE

BY

MICHAEL TOPOLOS

&

BETTY DOPSON

ARTWORK BY

SEBASTIAN TITUS

VINTAGE IMAGE & NAPA VALLEY

NAPA VALLEY

This book is dedicated to the colorful
men of the Napa Valley, past and
present, humble and great, who
loved the land, preserved its integrity,
and, out of toil and dreams, built
a wine empire in this place.

TABLE OF CONTENTS

Looking west across the valley from Howell Mt.

A WINE VALLEY IS BORN

Napa County, with its fertile valley edged with dramatic hills, looks much like the Bordeaux section of France. It has a long and fascinating geologic history.

Its marine sediments were formed millions of years ago, in the Jurassic period and up to Miocene times, when the area was ocean bed. Sedimentary rocks exposed in Napa Valley during the transformation period are mostly sandstone, silts, limestones, cherts and conglomerates. Sandstone predominates; it is often mistakenly referred to by the wineries as limestone.

The valley was raised from the primordial sea, along with the rest of the continent. Slow yet tremendous pressures of the earth rising and folding caused sedimentary formations to bend and crack; volcanic action erupted, spewing extensively, burying earlier sedimentary crust under hundreds of feet of ash and lava. Molten glass poured from the earth, forming the obsidian outcroppings seen today on Glass Mountain, along Silverado Trail. These deposits were much valued by Indians for arrow tips and spear points.

These turbulences lasted for centuries, and gave a great variety of minerals. Aluvial deposits washed down from elevations, creating a fertile valley, covered with trees and lush vegetation where game abounded. It was crossd by creeks and rivers, teeming with fish.

Thus, through the happen-chance of Nature, a realm of unique beauty and utility to man was created. To its borders came migrations of Indian tribes, and the history of its human civilization began.

No story of the valley can be told without giving a prominent place to its Indian tribes. Although recent census figures show a present day Indian population of 215 persons, they lived here in thousands, in harmony with Nature, no less than 4000 years ago, as testified by the mummified body of an Indian girl, found in the Angwin area at the turn of the century. Arthur Atwood excavated the burial mound, which contained the body completely preserved in five layers of buckskin and pitch, "in a sitting position, knees tucked up with her arms around them." Carbon test determined the age of the body to be approximately 4000 years. Dr. Robert Heizer states in his "Anthropological Records" that a Glass Mountain excavation site implies occupation by Indian tribes at least 2000 years B. C.

The Indians were blessed with a life of beauty, simplicity and peace. They were natural conservationists, killing game as needed, drying the surplus for future use. They harvested acorns, berries and bulbs, to be eaten fresh and dried, realizing that some must be left to insure future crops. They wove beautiful baskets, lined with pitch for cooking.

These humble "digger" Indians were not inferior people of low intelligence, but survived in their society by knowledge and skills. They used a long digging stick to harvest their foods from the ground, hence the epithet "digger." The men hunted and fished, making camps

Mt. St. Helena marks the valley's northern limit.

a short distance from spots where game was plentiful.

The sweathouse or temescal was the cultural center of each village. Here education, banquets, ceremonies and even hospitals brought the tribe together. Sweathouses were crudely-made oval structures of branches and mud, with a hole in the roof for smoke to escape.

The Wappos and Patwins comprised the largest groups of Indians. They had few cultural differences. The most evident of these was the ability of the more peaceful Patwins to ally themselves with the Mexican population, to the detriment of the neighboring Wappos. The Patwins had tribelets and settlements at Soscol, southeast Napa (Tulukai), and Napa (Termenukme). The Wappos were in Yountville (Kaimus), St. Helena (Annakatanoma) and the Hot Springs (Calistoga) area (Maiyakma, Niklektsonoma and Tselmenan).

Napa Valley Indians were clean, bathing daily, using the sweathouse and a fresh stream alternately. They had a high moral conscience, were religious, law abiding and aware of the importance of education. The young were taught the value of their cultural heritage, and a reverence for Nature. The name they gave this area was Ta-La-Ha-Lu-Si, translated "beautiful land," bespeaking their appreciation of esthetic values. Their most serious fault appears to have been their inability to adjust to the life styles of the white men who invaded this Eden.

The 10,000 to 12,000 Indians who lived here in 1831 dwindled during the next hundred years to a tenth of that number. Cholera epidemics and smallpox took most of their lives; many were lost during attacks by white men, who looked with indifference and contempt on them as beings of a lower order.

The Mexican revolt from Spain encouraged settlement to the North, and exploration and settlement of Napa Valley was part of this northward sweep. The Russian colony at Fort Ross posed a threat to the Mexican expansion, and Mexico, Russia and the USA vied with the Indians for possession of the area. The Mexicans, armed with their missions and militia, won out.

Mariano Vallejo had the resources to conquer, and in June 1823 the first expedition entered the valley. Mission San Rafael had been established six years earlier; another mission site was sought to the north. An armed escort led by Francisco Castro and Jose Sanchez left San Francisco and traveled to the areas of Petaluma, Napa, Sonoma and Suisun. Father Jose Altimira, after surveying these sites, chose to plant his mission cross in the Valley of the Moon, the twenty-first and final of the early Missions. Mission San Francisco Solano de Sonoma, 150 years later, is a familiar Sonoma landmark.

Although Napa Valley did not have a mission, it is indebted to Fr. Altamira for something quite different —a heritage of vines, olive and fig trees, and a golden trail of mustard.

It was the policy of the mission fathers that Indians should be rounded up, baptized and put to work for the Church. On the secular side, the Mexican government was giving out generous land grants to loyal citizens who would help to settle and expedite the expansion of their northern empire.

In the early 1830's, Napa Valley was a wild, adventurous land, attracting settlers from the east who had

Looking west off Zinfandel Lane.

conquered one wilderness and sought another. George Calvert Yount came to the valley from South Carolina in 1831, becoming a hunter, trapper and friend of General Vallejo. His deeds of valor, as a pioneer, soldier and frontiersman, made him the most colorful American ever to ride into Napa Valley. He journeyed over the Indian trail to the top of Mount St. Helena, rising nearly 5000 feet at the head of the valley. Turning to look at the panorama below, with its ribbon of gold-blossoming mustard, he said, "In such a place I should love to clear the land and make my home; in such a place I should love to live and die." He fulfilled his vision, living there until his death in 1865.

The years between were eventful and exciting. He hunted sea otters along the coast. He visited the Petaluma adobe of General Vallejo as Indians were puddling clay for roof tiles, and told the General of his ability to make shingles. "What are they?" asked Vallejo. Yount took his axe and demonstrated the merits of redwood shingles, which pleased the General with their lightness and durability. Yount hired Charles Brown, recently arrived from the whaler "Helvetius," paying him $25 a month, plus room and board, for his services. Together they cut the trees, barking them, splitting them into eighteen inch blocks, then into shingles. Each could make about 1000 shingles a day. Vallejo was pleased when the job was finished, and offered Yount land in payment, since coin was scarce. Yount accepted readily, saying "Half a league will do."

The General's domain was vast, stretching to the Sierras. "We do not deal in half leagues here," he said. "You will take four leagues." "One league," Yount countered, for even this would require a score of Indians to manage and work it, and his sole capital was his axe. "Two leagues, nothing less," said the General in a firm voice. "You will take all of Caymus Ranch." So Yount became a Roman Catholic, baptized Jorge Concepcion Yount, and a Mexican citizen. Having fulfilled these requirements, the land grant was finalized, consisting of 11,814.52 acres in the heart of Napa Valley. His only neighbors were Indians. He built the first wooden structure in the county, a two-story Kentucky block house with portholes for protection against unfriendly Indians.

Yount understood and respected Indians; there was always a free exchange of information between them, to the betterment of both. Indians worked well for him, helping with improvements on his property. He planted vineyards, taking his grapes to Vallejo's winery; he raised sheep, horses and cattle, maintained fruit orchards, built a flour mill and a sawmill, and provided hospitality in the grand manner for all newcomers.

Yount's friendliness went ill requited. After the Land Act of 1851 threw titles of existing Mexican grant holders into confusion, squatters overran the valley. He claimed they caused him more trouble than Indians and grizzly bears combined. They took possession of his land, stole his cattle and fruit from his orchards, while he paid the taxes. Later, in 1855, the US government confirmed his Mexican title to the land.

After his death at 71 years of age, the name of the town, formerly called Sebastopol, was changed to Yountville in his honor. He can truly be called the father of Napa Valley.

The old Bale Mill north of St. Helena.

The early 1840's found many immigrants arriving, farmers, not pioneers, interested in the plow rather than the axe. They could get land in three ways—perform services for it, buy it, or squat on it. They brought problems, challenged land grants, built fences. The land was very fertile, the wild oats growing above the back of a horse. It was studded with oaks, the habitat of elk, deer and bear.

Cattle were raised for food, but more importantly for hides and tallow. Large herds developed the first industry in the valley—tanning. The oak bark was taken from valley trees, and cured hides became a valuable export.

Equally as important were grapes. The Mission grape was planted on the ranches by the settlers; Indians trampled the grapes in a hide trough with bare feet, and the wine was fermented in skin bags.

Fenced farms began chopping up the land. The first major crop was wheat, reaped with a rough sickle, dried a day or two, and then horses were driven over it to thrash out the grain. Flour mills were erected, the remaining one being the Bale Mill, and sawmills were built for lumber taken from mountains and hillsides. Towns cropped up, and the Mexican Rancho period was ended; the era of agriculture began.

The 1840's marked an influx of covered wagon pioneers. History records that many members of the Bidwell-Bartelson party purchased land in the upper valley, as did settlers of the Grigsby-Ide party, between 1841 and 1845. Many of them returned East in a few years, claiming that all of the good land was gone and there was no opportunity.

Squabbles between contenders for the land, burnings, gunfights and Indian battles marked the beginning of the agricultural era. When the Gold Rush came, 49ers flooded the valley and left their impact on it. Gold fever sent many valley dwellers to the Motherlode to try their luck; many chose to return to their farms and extract their gold from successful miners wintering in the valley. Prices soared; the sale of two acres of onions brought $8000 to the farmer. William H. Nash, a horticulturist near Calistoga, sold his first peach crop, 100 peaches, for $100. Who needed a mine?

Development of vineyards on a commercial scale began in the late 1800's, after experimentation with wheat, barley and oats. Corn, potatoes, melons, pears, peaches, apples and grapes were grown on the ranchos, and oranges, olives, prunes and even tobacco were tried in this period.

The wealth of San Francisco at its feet and the success of vines in Sonoma County, augmented by the falling price of wheat, prompted the planting of the vine in Napa County. A table of profit in 1881 from two acres shows: Barley, $15.50; Wheat, $16.80; Corn, $27.25; Vines, $252.35.

The market for wine seemed unquenchable. Less fertile land in the valley, found to be unsuited to orchards and grains, proved valuable for vines. Men impressed with the valley came with wine on their minds, and set out to plant the available land. The state government aided them with research, publications, commissions and tax advantages. New vineyards were exempt from taxes for four years. Enthusiasm reigned.

Thanks to the colorful Count Agostin **Haraszthy**,

Old La Perla Winery atop Spring Mountain.

the European varieties were introduced about 1860. All but five of the 49 winemakers in 1879 were men of wealth, from European winemaking backgrounds. Prior to that time, wine made was of the Mission type. By 1867 there were 1000 acres in cultivation, with over 750,000 vines. The largest vineyard, owned by Sam Brannan, was 125,000 vines; the second was the Crane estate, with 62,000.

There was no stopping the flood tide; by 1881 there were 433 vineyards in the three districts of Napa, St. Helena and Calistoga, covering 11,043 acres. Ten years later there were 619 vineyards on more than 17,000 acres.

Early winemaking was primitive. The wine only satisfied local consumption; Idwal Jones reported of the Mission grape: "It was mediocre but useful, and the Franciscans wrought their honest best with it." But it was obvious that the future of valley wine did not lie there.

Charles Krug was the first to make non-Mexican wine in the county. In 1858, with his cider press and European wine knowhow, he proved a fine wine could be made from valley grapes.

Figures show the following rate of growth:

YEAR	GALLONS OF WINE
1860	8,520
1870	297,070
1880	2,460,000
1890	4,252,000

This increase brought on an overexpansion of vineyards and winemaking in the middle 1870's, and this, coupled with the Depression of 1874-77, sent many growers into bankruptcy. The industry was shocked, and began an effort toward planting improved European varieties, using new techniques of winemaking, which led to further expansion until the 1890 Depression sent the price of grapes to $8 a ton. This, coupled with phylloxera, knocked the growers to their knees, and gave the industry a blow from which it took years to recover.

Growers could not believe their vineyards were infected with the dread phylloxera, a disease without a remedy. It destroyed 10,000 acres; production fell from four million gallons in 1890 to two million in 1892. and to 407,612 gallons by the time it bottomed out in 1899.

The cure for the dread disease was found to consist of grafting to Vitis Riparia or Rupestus roots, and although financial losses had beggared many, the industry began to recover. New plainting were of superior varieties, and this created a sound basis for the agricultural community.

No sooner had the industry recovered than Prohibition came into the picture in 1919, with consequent closing of wineries and pulling out of vineyards. Many held on; no Italian, recalls an oldtimer, ever believed such an unnatural law could last. Until Repeal in 1933, a few wineries existed by making and selling sacramental wines; some shut down and let wineries fall into decline; vines were replaced by other crops. A few went on making and selling wine via the bootleg route, surviving by fair means or foul until the inexplicable madness was over.

Then came years of building back. A vineyard,

The old Occidental winery built in 1878.

like Rome, is not built in a day. Thus, instead of 200 years of solid, smooth advancement, the industry in Napa Valley can look back only about 40 years, a short time indeed in wine history compared with European centuries of developing and improving wines and vines.

In the history of the valley, a few names loom large. Among them are Jacob Schram, Gustave Niebaum, Jacob and Frederick Beringer, Charles Krug, Georges deLatour. These men came to the valley, some from affluence, some from poverty, with a dream so vast that to give their whole lives to its achievement seemed a privilege rather than a price to pay. They created a wine empire, built for the future, saw greatness ahead for valley wines. They lived as they made wine, with elegance and style, and their wineries have become valley shrines.

In the chronicles of the valley another people had an impact on the land—the Chinese. Almost none of them existed in the USA before 1850; then lured by visions of gold to be picked up in the streets they came to California, and remained to become the labor force behind the building of the wine empire.

They dug tunnels, made stone walls, toiled in orchards and vineyards, unhonored, unsung, little appreciated, often exploited. The 500 or so Chinese in Napa County left their mark on the valley; it can be seen today. The tunnels they dug, the walls they built, are humble monuments to a people who toiled long and hard, poorly paid, often treated with disrespect, yet always maintaining their own culture and self-respect. They are gone, but their influence lingers in the land they helped to build.

The history of the wine industry in Napa Valley has been a story of ups and downs, with very little time spent on middle ground. A legacy of growth and decline has culminated in the present building up on sound economic principles. Perhaps this has all contributed to character in the wine; if the industry had not suffered these series of traumas and triumphs, the wine might not be as good as it is today, for the best wine comes from the vine that must work harder to produce its grapes. To continue the analogy, it is doubtful if any valley winemaker today would admit to a life of luxury and ease.

Cabernet Sauvignon cluster.

NOBLE VINES & VINEYARDS

The story of wine begins in the vineyard. Vines are esthetically pleasing, and their abundance makes Napa Valley a refreshing sea of green in a dry California summer. On close scrutiny, each wine stands out and has its own personality, for grape varieties differ from one another and are individuals.

It is a fortunate fact that when vines go into an area, it inhibits housing tracts, and means that, for years ahead, the integrity of the land will be preserved, pleasing the senses and adding to man's well-being. Everyone recalls when Santa Clara Valley, a gloriously fertile area, was paved over—one of the finest pieces of agricultural land in the world was lost. With today's prospect of food shortage, this fact becomes alarming.

Here in Napa County, 25,000 acres are included in the Agricultural Preserve, created by an act of the County Board of Supervisors. Depending for its life on their action, it prevents the sale of land within its confines in small blocks, restricting it to tracts twenty acres in extent. The Preserve was enacted at a strategic moment in the life of the valley, in 1968, and has set a pattern for other areas wishing to keep urban encroachment at bay.

The life cycle of a vineyard is attuned to seasonal change, with each season bringing its own phase of plant life. After the harvest in August, September and October, the vine rests from its labors and gathers strength for another growing season. Growers always want sufficient cold to force dormancy in early winter, but this is rarely a problem in Napa Valley. Dormant vines are busy storing carbohydrates, getting ready, after hibernation, for a great thrust forward. Meanwhile the grower has time to work on his equipment and rest up for spring tasks; perhaps take a vacation.

In spring, the first warmth wakens the vine and starts its sap flowing. Its energies are high after a long rest, and it is ready to respond to pruning as weather permits workers to enter the vineyard. The pruning technique is one well-known method of quality control through limiting quantity. Before Pasteur's discovery of acetobacter, the effects of oxygen on wine, it was the most vital factor in wine production.

Pruning is always a hand operation, and the hand must be expert, for on the pruner's judgment hangs the quality of the crop. Cutting too heavily reduces potential tonnage. Insufficient pruning fails to insure proper bearing on the canes, involving the risk of overcropping, when the vine may produce more fruit than it can ripen. Competence here is vital to the vine's well-being and longevity.

Vines have a long life, from 90 to 100 years, and some vineyards in commercial bearing in Napa Valley are fifty and sixty years old. However, with the utmost in yield becoming daily more important, for reasons of economics, growers today plan to replant every 30 to 40 years.

When the ground is relatively dry, equipment is

Ancient Zinfandel vine.

moved into the vineyard to turn under the cover crop. This puts nitrogen into the soil, and exposes the vine to maximum sunshine. It also gets rid of plants that compete with the vine for moisture and nutrients.

The greatest threat of spring is frost, which can cut potential tonnage drastically during the flowing season. Fortunes have been spent installing permanent-set irrigation systems, heaters and aeroplane engines to warm and circulate the air and prevent temperature drop below the critical 32 degrees.

Permanent-set irrigation requires large resources of water, which is not in plentiful supply here and often must be developed. But it is very effective in inhibiting frost damage. Water is sprayed on vines during frost periods and allowed to freeze; conversion into ice generates heat. A continual spray keeps water freezing and releasing its heat until frost danger is past. Severe winds and hail can also deplete potential tonnage by knocking flowers from vines before berry set.

Dusting is another important spring task; controlling fungus and organisms harmful to the development of the crop. Growth below the head must also be removed by suckering, to direct the vine's energy into balanced production. As the season advances, more spraying and cultivating may be necessary. It is vital for the vine to be able to photosynthesize enough sunshine to nurture and mature the crop.

Now the urgent chores are done, and the grower waits for the grapes to ripen. U. C. Davis designates a 214-day growing season, April 1 to October 31, for crop development. In Napa Valley, ripening of the crop is seldom a problem; what European grapes lack in sunshine is more than made up here. But in Europe, in a years with more than usual sunshine, there occurs one of those great vintages that produce noble wines, for grapes are able to develop more sugar, and thus more alcohol, body and character.

During the growing season, the grower must observe the grapes closely and test them frequently, for as sugar increases, acid decreases, and a most important factor in winemaking is proper sugar-acid balance.

The late summer ripening period is an extremely critical time, for now birds and deer begin to take their toll of the crop. Deer can jump a ten-foot fence to feast on the vines, and migrations of Starling populations from Oregon and Washington are monitored daily. These birds travel in flocks of thousands, and each bird can eat a pound of grapes per day. Vigilance on the part of the grower is at an all-season high during this pre-harvest period.

Fall brings the climax of the grape growing year; now weather is all-important, for untimely rain can lower sugar content by dilution, and can also produce mildew and mold. Workers move into the vineyards and the crop is picked diligently, for getting the grapes off the vine and to the crusher at the right time, and in good condition, is vital to making good wine.

Along with the cycle of seasons, there are other influences in the life of the vine: Soil, climate, grape variety and man.

Soil is basically an anchor for the vine, performing three functions: Depth sufficient for root penetration: Nutrients, and Water Retention Capability. With modern technology such as drip irrigation, soil depth is not

Chardonnay grape cluster.

an all-important criterion in selecting a vineyard site. If soil lacks nutrients such as nitrogen, these can be provided with minimal problems.

Vines will grow in almost any soil; less well in heavy clay and in soils containing alkali salts. Heavy crops are produced on deep, fertile soil, but surprisingly enough, grape quality is better on soils of poorer fertility.

Vine roots penetrate the soil to a depth of about ten feet, and once a vineyard is established, it needs only about 20 inches of rain each year. Average rainfall in Napa Valley is 30 to 40 inches.

Soils vary from rich and deep to shallow and poor. Some vineyards are dry, and have no irrigation water, while others have drainage problems that must be corrected with drain tile systems. Most are non-irrigated, but water is always needed to get young vines established.

In some areas there are problems due to high winter and spring water table, which restricts root growth. Too much boron is a problem in some areas; dificiency of boron in others. Winter growth or cover crops supply some of the nitrogen needed for good production, and most vineyards do not receive additional fertilizers.

In Europe, food supply had to be considered before vines, with valleys left to grow grains and grapes planted on hillsides of necessity. This Italian and French influence came to California along with the wine grapes, bringing the idea that quality grapes must grow on hillsides to duplicate conditions under which fine wine is produced in Europe.

Many Napa Valley growers dry farm their vineyards and believe in the superiority of this method with an almost religious zeal, tending to frown on those who resort to irrigation to get bigger crops. Vineyards with sprinkler systems use them mainly for frost control, and to cool vines on days of extreme heat.

It is true that the more a vine must struggle to survive, the more character it will pick up along the way. It will be noted that the very fertile valleys of the San Joaquin produce bountiful crops of splendid-looking grapes, which, because of heat and fertility, are lacking in acid and character. This stems from a large skin-to-pulp ratio which tends to dilute flavor and odor constituents. Happily, soil and climate in Napa Valley are just the right combination to produce this desired character.

The climate of the valley, with its warm days and cool nights during the growing season, is recognized everywhere as growing incomparable grapes, with good sugar-acid balance and the character produced by just the right amount of stress. It is impossible to over-emphasize the impact of the micro-climate in this area; Keith Bowers, Napa County farm advisor, puts it this way: "Each grape has a micro-climate in the cluster."

Fitting grape variety to micro-climate is constantly being studied. With current grape prices, growers can afford to tear out old, spotty planting, replacing them with those exactly right for the location, and much of this has been done in the past few years.

Napa County lies in U. C. Davis-designated Zones I, II and III, but a more realistic division is into four major plant-climates, which may be classified as Maritime, Coastal, Transitional and Interior, depending on the degree of ocean influence.

Winter vineyards off Langtry Rd.

The Maritime area includes the section lying southwest of the city of Napa. Here the day vs. night temperature is a narrow range, as is seasonal change. Summer fog is characteristic of this section, known as Los Carneros, and it is best suited for early ripening grapes such as Pinot Noir and Chardonnay.

The Coastal zone extends from Napa to just north of St. Helena, and from the foothills on the east to the Sonoma County line on the west. As is typical of Napa Valley micro-climates, this can be subdivided into a cooler southern section, Napa to Yountville, and a warmer section north of the summer fog line of the Yountville hills. Going up the valley the climate gets warmer, for due to ocean influence, the south end of the county is, climatically, the north.

This Coastal zone is suited to growing both early and late maturing varietals of the finest quality, and is often called "Cabernet Country." The viticulturist-winemaster Andre Tchelistcheff says: "Cabernet needs Rutherford dust," and it is to this noble grape that most of the new plantings in this area are now devoted.

Beginning north of St. Helena at Lodi Lane on the south boundary, and extending to the town of Calistoga on the north, lies the Transitional zone, best suited to the later-maturing varieties.

The Pope, Berryessa and Chiles Valley areas are in the Interior zone, which is least influenced by cool ocean air and dominated by continental air. However, many other climatic influences bear on the micro-climate. Elevation and exposure of hillside vineyards in these valleys tend to influence interior valley heat toward coolness.

Rainfall varies in the different zones, with about 20 inches at Napa, 30 inches in the center of the valley, and up to 50 inches in the foothills. The temperature curve is another factor—if the temperature reaches 90 degrees in the daytime, it will be about 45 degrees at night, and this proportion, necessary for quality grape production, is almost constantly maintained.

The many small micro-climatic differences due to exposure, air, drainage and elevation each play a part in influencing the grapes. It can be said that everything in the environment influences the grapes.

There are now in Napa County 19,953 acres of bearing and non-bearing vineyard, with much of the planting done in the past eight to ten years. Great care has been taken to match grape variety to micro-climate, section by section, and much work and experimentation have been devoted to selecting superior stock. Isolating and propagating disease-resistant strains of varietal grape vines is a business of maximum proportions, and great stress is laid on locating and propagating clonal strains which have shown greater qualities of hardiness and plant vigor. Large scale methods of bench grafting and heat propagation of vines have been developed to insure a sufficient supply of young grape stock to meet the demand. All this is done to insure that, with proper handling, grapes will produce distinguished wines.

UC Davis has crossed varieties that grow best in this area to provide new hybrids that grow well and develop character in the state's big valleys, with considerable success. But it has been demonstrated that they can only approach, never equal, the noble varietals that Napa Valley grows superlatively well, such as Cabernet

The valley in Spring seen from Silverado Trail.

Sauvignon, Pinot Noir, Chardonnay and White Riesling. Except for the native areas in Europe which developed them, these grapes are unsurpassed when grown in this small area of California.

The last great influence on the grapes is man himself—the man who plants, grows and cultivates the crop. Decisions made by the grower, month by month, year by year, have a profound effect on the vineyard. Vineyard management is anything the grower cares to make it, and his decisions make or mar the grapes on which quality of wine depends. This is no field for amateurs, but for skilled and dedicated technicians.

Man's influence on the land cannot be dealt with in depth without acknowledging our debt to the Indian, Chinese and Mexican laborers who helped build California's wine country. These people, of humble origin, had an affinity for the soil, and a commitment, inherent in their culture, to preserve and enhance the land, which those who come after them might well emulate.

The harvest is a very special event in wine country, the culmination of an entire year of effort. Picking grapes is a pleasure; the weather is warm, with fall in the air. The whole countryside turns out and works with a will, growers and their families bending to the task beside the hired pickers. It is a magical time, with the light-hearted gaiety of Christmas, and bringing a heightened awareness and quickened pace that sets it apart from the rest of the year.

Unlike any other crop, the life of a grape begins at harvest, and may go on for years, whereas other crops decline, and never become more and better than they are at harvest. With grapes, there is always a potential for something more. Each cluster picked will become a few sips of wine—perhaps great wine. This is an inspiring thought, and makes the labor of harvest light and big with hope.

Los Carneros vineyards below Miliken Peak.

The Napa Valley Today

Many new names and faces have appeared in Napa Valley's wine picture in recent months, all fired with a determination to produce the finest quality wines possible.

One of the facts of life today is the corporate ownership of many of the wineries, old and new; the reason for this is one of economics. The large holdings of family-owned land that exist elsewhere throughout the world are virtually impossible here. The European tradition of the eldest son retaining the holdings of the family has served to keep the large tracts of land intact abroad.

Here, whenever land passes down in the family, it must be split up or merged with a larger company. This fact is responsible for breaking family traditions of winemaking, and has prompted corporate ownership of winery facilities as the only way of survival. Good, bad or indifferent, this is what is happening today.

If a winery reaches a certain level of production, it is virtually impossible for it to remain in family ownership, unless the family has very deep roots. Corporations come on the scene, offering vast amounts of money to enter this romantic, and currently very lucrative, field. The incongruity lies in the fact that a small producer also has a place on the wine scene. Many of them in the industry today gain at least as much satisfaction from producing fine wines as they do from producing a living.

A winery's product can be only as good as the grapes used to make it. With fine grapes at a premium, most facilities in the valley are dependent on their own vineyard holdings. At one time it was considered necessary for a winery to maintain production of a full range of wines, but with today's orientation toward specialization, the smaller producers are concentrating only on the wines they can produce best. They leave it to the large, corporately owned wineries to produce the entire gamut of wine varieties.

At the turn of the century there were 142 wineries in the valley, nearly one hundred over today's figure. At that time, almost everyone who grew grapes made wine in his own winery, and the valley is studded with the remains of small stone wineries, dug into hillsides, now picturesque ruins.

Although some wineries are not accessible to the general public, most will, either by appointment or by just dropping in, accommodate an interested visitor. The hospitality that reigns in the valley is refreshing and reassuring. The wineries offering their wares at no expense to visitors can give a cordial and pleasing introduction to a wine.

There is something very special about drinking wine where it is made. After all, wine is a reflection of a mingling of sun, soil and man. There is an aura at the winery that makes it impossible to be indifferent to the wine, and sipping wine while surrounded by the barrels, crushers and presses, inhaling the winery breath that

West Slope seen from Larkmead Lane.

steals from walls and ceilings, inextricably binds one to the moment. It is not unusual for a wine that sharply delights at the winery to become somewhat dull when it is uncorked at home. This reinforces the French concept that wine should be drunk where it is made.

The fame of Napa Valley is not merely recognized locally, but is becoming world-wide. In "The Wines of America," Leon D. Adams recognizes it as "the winiest county," and Frona Eunice Wait, in "Wines and Vines of California" (1889), devotes a large part of the book to Napa Valley and its wines and wineries.

Our European forebears did not settle the valley and bring their vines by mistake, or by accident. Their background of winemaking revealed to them that the area had all the constituents of great wine country, and the wines made here have mirrored this truth. Now we find even the chauvinistic French, who scoff at almost any wine not originating within the confines of their own country, aggressively planting vines in Napa Valley. If imitation is the sincerest form of flattery, what better, more flattering, tribute could a winegrowing area receive than this?

Bearing out the contention that it is the people as much as anything else that make the valley great wine country, these newcomers, its most ardent world competitors in wine, are being welcomed with open arms and open minds.

Napa Valley is great wine country because its people are great, quite as much as because of climatic factors. The gods were kind to Napa Valley; its climate is a special variant of Mediterranean, with warm, dry summer days cooled with fog from San Pablo Bay at the south, giving life-saving coolness to vines on hottest summer days. A fortuitous combination of soil and climate make grapes grown here superior in flavor to any grown elsewhere on this continent.

But more is involved than physical characteristics. Wine-making is a matter here of honor and pride. The old-time wine men understood this well; to them, no investment of time and money was too great to achieve excellence. They knew that the truth is in the glass, and that no amount of sales promotion weighs against the product itself. Theirs is a proud tradition, and it is a vital part of winemaking here today.

For the past hundred years, a winery has been an expression of its owner's pride and integrity, a tribute to the best we mean when we say "the American way of life." It stands for something in the national character, for the people of this country, this state and this valley do have a culture, and it is a fine one.

As a people, Californians have dipped heavily into their European origins, but they have also found their own identity on this land. Their wine has tremendous strength, concentration of flavor and odors, which might seem crass to an European's pedigreed palate. But it is their own, having in abundance the strength and vigor of youth. The wine made here, for the most part, is honest wine, with power in it, plus the compelling charm of vitality and youth.

Today there is a place in the industry for anyone to plant a vineyard with superior clonal strains of the great varieties suited to his particular micro-climates, make wine according to his own standards, knowledge, dedication and expertise, and stand on the statement he has

The valley's northernmost vineyard.

made. He can market it to people who care about the things he values and strives to achieve and maintain. It is still, as in the time of Captain Niebaum, the most rewarding way of life conceivable for one who loves the land, enjoys enhancing the gifts of Nature, has the infinite capacity for taking pains that winemaking demands, plus that sixth sense, winewise, that tells him when to let the wine alone to be itself. Could any life offer more?

In our society, as affluence increases, money loses its importance as a status symbol, and its place is taken by creativity. We are more and more drawn to creative workers who do their own work superlatively well, and do it in their own fashion. The winegrower and winemaker has the supreme opportunity to do this.

Competition among valley winemakers is keen, but rivalry is never such that a neighbor vintner cannot be called upon in time of need. Many of the wine men of the valley are noted for their diligence in aiding, with good advice, encouragement and in more tangible ways, those newcomers to the scene who will some day compete with them in the market place.

A visit to a winery is always a pleasure. In summer, many wineries offer picnic facilities, besides streams or lakes, or overlooking a spectacular view. There, under shady trees on a languid summer day, luncheon may be enjoyed with a bottle of crisply cool wine.

In fall, the slow-paced valley comes to life with bustle and hurry to get grapes picked and to the crusher at the moment of greatest flavor. Vines put on dress of red, purple and gold to celebrate the vintage, and after the grapes are in there is a time of relaxation and feasting as one busy year ends and another, bumper to bumper, begins, for the calendar of wine stretches from vintage to vintage.

Here wine is an important adjunct to life, as it was in the past, and dining is an art. Along with great wine, many homes make a point of great cuisine. Here the food is like the best wine, with the same casual elegance. It has an international flavor that owes something to Italian, French, Swiss, Portuguese, German, Spanish and Russian tradition, plus perhaps a dash of the Oriental. With this rich heritage to draw upon, food selection and preparation ranks right along with selecting the right wine for an occasion. No wine country hostess hesitates to spend the needed hours in this creative pursuit.

Wine is a life style as well as a livelihood. It has permeated every strata of our society, from the student quaffing and sharing his bottle with his peers at a "happening," to the vintner of stature entertaining distinguished, cosmopolitan wine men at his table, spending an hour, or two or three, choosing wines from his private cellar for their pleasure.

Every cellar has its quota of Napa Valley wine, rubbing shoulders with the great imported wines. The cocktail hour has been largely edged out by the wine and cheese party in this wine-oriented spot. Seldom is there good conversation of an evening that does not turn at some time to the wines of the area, with lively discussions of their merit, and the colorful people, past and present who made them.

The greatness of the valley people extends to all who live here. Whether directly connected with winemaking or not, they feel themselves a proud part of the wine.

Pritchard Hill vineyards overlooking Lake Hennessy.

A LOOK AT THE FUTURE

To estimate the future is to survey our knowledge of the past. The current emphasis on wine makes the probability of overplanting in Napa Valley a subject of discussion whenever two wine men meet; history has a way of repeating itself, and the booms and busts of the valley's past have left their mark on the wine community.

The industry, banks, lending institutions and agricultural economists have all taken a whirl at predicting what lies ahead. Their views have been extremely optimistic, up to the present and a few years beyond. Winemakers and growers are delighted; they see nothing but expansion and success ahead, for the balance of this century. They are probably right—AS LONG AS THEY PLACE THE PROPER EMPHASIS ON QUALITY.

Wine growing and winemaking as a life style offer much. Wine Consultant Brad Webb, who has guided many valley wine enterprises through their first critical years, says: "At the time I came to the valley (1947), being a winemaker had no more prestige than being a shoemaker." The situation is dramatically reversed today; a winemaker is accorded tremendous respect, and a fine winemaker is looked upon almost with reverence.

It is not surprising, under the circumstances, that hundreds of enterprising people arrive in the valley each year, eager to ride to success on this wave of the future. But it is also certain that all who embark will not arrive.

Just a few years ago, wine consumption in this country was around two gallons per capita annually. As late as a year ago it was around four gallons. If one drank a tenth of wine a day, he would consume 36 gallons annually. Most California wine drinkers consume this much, but it is fantastically in excess of the national, even the state, average, more like figures for France or Italy.

People will continue to have an appetite for wine and the money to gratify it, for income is expected to go up along with population growth. As prices rise, better wine continues to find a ready sale. Probably all the output in the valley could be sold in the immediate area, but most Napa Valley vintners have opted for national distribution. They want all to know the valley wines, and to concur in their belief that this favored strip of land is destined to become a second Cote d'Or.

Attention is focused on the industry, with outsiders yearning to get in, and insiders using every management tactic and skill to keep costs down, production at a profitable level, and to adopt advantageous business practices so they need fear no competition. In reality, makers of fine wine are plagued with competition in the same way as two artists selling their wares, for wine is more than a mere product.

Market trends are being studied with diligence by agricultural economists. For the next few years, it appears likely that the rate of crush increase will lag behind the rate of wine shipment increase, which leads them to believe that continued strong prices are certain. This

Manicured vineyards along the West Slope.

does not mean that growers and winemakers can now relax and enjoy their affluence, for supply is bound to exceed demand at some point, and the industry will be on the roller coaster once more.

But, with current knowledge and constant study by those involved with the industry, there will be little excuse for this if it does happen. It will be because they have ignored the signals, for if knowledge is power, never before have vintners been so well equipped to handle their problems.

Wine promotion has been low key, involving people slowly but surely. Wine and food groups have sprung up everywhere; wine appreciation courses, wine articles, wine columns, wine consumer magazines, wine cookbooks, are increasing in number and scope each year. Retail shops devoted exclusively to the sale of wine are springing up like mushrooms after a rain.

This is all promotion. It did not happen overnight, nor by accident. Greater affluence, with the consequent increase in travel and social occasions, has opened new vistas on the world of wine. The "new" consumer with an informed taste for good wine did not just suddenly appear, as Agricultural Economist Dr. Kirby Moulton says, "like Venus on the half-shell." He is the result of quiet but persistent industry promotion.

Dr. Moulton declares: "There is no magic in bigness." In the making of fine wine, the small operator has a distinct advantage over the large operator in terms of quality, and this is where we came in. Quality is still and above all the answer. Nobody needs a crystal ball to predict that quality wines will never be oversupplied. If we keep our sights high, overproduction just can't

happen in Napa Valley—there isn't that much land.

A dramatic series of events that influenced the future of the valley began in 1964 with the sale of Inglenook to United Vintners, a large corporation and subsidiary of Heublein Inc. In 1969, Beaulieu was sold directly to Heublein, and in 1970 Beringer Brothers sold out the third of the beautiful historic valley wineries to a food chain, Nestle Inc.

These events marked a change in the life of Napa Valley, and established a future along very different lines. It is a change from a culture and way of life predominantly rural, intimate and tied to the land. Time has finally caught up with Napa Valley and altered its slow-paced way of life.

Will corporate ownership and expansion continue? Will more of the family owned wineries go the corporate ownership route? Only time and chance can tell. The owners of Beringer Winery now have a $20 million expansion of facilities across the highway from the winery. United Vintners, owners of Inglenook, have just completed construction of a several-building complex at the front of the original winery.

Heads of the wineries remaining in family hands intend to carry on in that way, resisting some enticing offers from big corporations to do so. Whether or not they can carry out their plans for the future depends on many factors, unforseeable at present.

It must be emphasized that, while expansion of plantings and winemaking may have reached the saturation point elsewhere, it does not seem to threaten here. It is currently hinted that some wineries have wines left unmarketed in the warehouse at the end of the season.

East slope Spring Vineyards near Calistoga.

However, the small, quality-oriented wineries have trouble supplying their customers. It has been said that there can never be too much good wine, and experience of these Napa Valley vintners seem to bear this out.

In agriculture as a whole, production problems have been largely solved or reduced to manageable size. It is management skills that control survival today in any branch of agriculture, and winemaking, for all its romantic image, is still agriculture.

When young vines come into commercial bearing, a few years of bumper grape crops would have an impact on price.

In considering the future of the valley, one sincerely interested in looking at reality must ask, what will happen here if the price of grapes should drop? Most growers remember the prices of the 30's and 40's; what if this should happen again? How many could survive with grapes at $100 or $200 a ton? Few would care to hazard a guess, but all agree that there would be casualties.

A great deal might be said on the contributions the big corporate interests have brought to the valley— maintaining the green belt, stabilizing prices, promoting the valley wines—and this fact is recognized and appreciated. But there remains an uneasy feeling that the slumbering volcano in our midst might not be extinct after all, and that people who live and make wine here occupy a position perilously near its edge. Constant vigilance and market awareness continue to be the constituents of successful winemaking, as well as quality.

However, of the moment all is well. The grower-vintner who loves the vine and its product, who enjoys making wine as a way of life, who finds an excitement in the challenge of producing better and ever better wines, and who will understand and utilize the tools of management and marketing, will continue to prosper doing the thing he loves to do. Many of them say they would make wine anyway, even if there were no money in it, for the sheer love of living in the wine country, the exhileration of being part of a vital and dynamic industry, and the gamble with Nature each year brings.

These small producers will continue to release a limited amount of good, very good and great wine each year. The best of it will probably command a rather fantastic price, so that those who are less than affluent will drink it on special occasions, going to the middle category of wineries to supply the daily bottle.

The undiscriminating or beginning wine drinker will, now and in the future, find plenty of drinkable Napa Valley wine at his price level, although this may involve the field of jug wines. If he continues to drink wine, read about it, listen to lectures and mingle with wine lovers, his tastes will change in an upward direction. He will save on other things to afford a case of a special Zinfandel he believes has possibilities, or a bottle or two of an elegant Cabernet.

To pinpoint events of the future with any degree of certainty is clearly impossible. But in a world of changing ideas and values, one dependable fact emerges: The number of informed wine drinkers is not going to decrease. Those who have made the acquaintance of wine have acquired an interest which will be with them forever, moving up from the status of a beverage to that of a life style and a dear and familiar friend.

THE WINERIES

CARNEROS CREEK WINERY

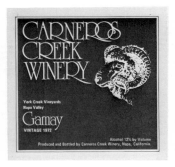

Carneros Creek Winery is situated beneath the slopes of Miliken Peak and is the southernmost winery in the valley. The owners, Balfour and Anita Gibson, founded the winery in 1971 and the licence is held by Connoisseur Wine Imports of San Francisco.

Los Carneros (the sheep) is the famous cool wine growing area close to San Pablo Bay where the early ripening varieties of grapes are particularly at home. The marine intrusion and fog factor play a vital role in the development of high quality varietal fruit. The varieties, Pinot Noir, Chardonnay and White Reisling, are able to stay on the vine in this area longer, retain their balance of sugar and acid and thus develop more character.

The basic premise of this winery is to help establish vineyards and plant the right varieties at the right places to achieve maximum results in the wine. This will require the diligence of Francis Mahoney, the winemaker, to oversee the vineyard operations during all phases of pruning, cultivation and picking, in this low Region I area.

Mahoney was an employee of the Gibsons in their importing business, and the three decided to establish a vineyard and begin making wine. He was already a home winemaker, with experience from working at Mayacamas, and he attacked the project with enthusiasm. "To put in 10 acres of vineyard with your own hands helps to destroy the romantic view," he comments, "and if that doesn't do it, then there is the hard, tiring work and long hours at winery chores that go on seven days a week." His first wine was made in a San Francisco basement in 1971. In spite of all this, the young winemaker is filled with zeal for the years ahead.

This grand experiment will be a five year program and the results are yet to be seen. The 1974 crush will include Cabernet Sauvignon from five different locations and as Mahoney relates "only the years will tell the future of these wines". It is a noble gesture to seek the finest wine obtainable. As the years go by and the experiment progresses, the reputation of Carneros Creek Winery is sure to increase.

The winery, completed in 1973, is constructed of Sonoma block and poured solid. The dimensions are 55 x 40 feet, and the roof has 6 inches of styrofoam. All of the fermenting is done outside in stainless steel, refrigerated fermentors that have been designed at a pitch of 3 inches to the foot to allow for ease of movement of the must.

The ultimate goal of the winery is to achieve a volume of between 5,000 and 10,000 cases a year. There are less than 10 acres at the winery site, recently budded to Pinot Noir, which will augment the other grapes that will be marketed. Cabernet Sauvignon, Pinot Chardonnay, Zinfandel and Pinot Noir will be made and sold by the winery in the near future with an emphasis on the Appelation and district recognition of individual vineyards.

There is no tasting or sales at the winery but an advance appointment should secure the interested visitor a delightful tour.

MT. VEEDER WINERY

This small winery is pleasantly situated on the slopes of Mt. Veeder at a level from 1000 to 1400 feet. It is the old Moyer place, purchased in 1963 by Michael and Arlene Bernstein as a summer home.

Ownership is a limited partnership formed in 1972, with attorney-viticulturist Michael Bernstein and Kimbal Giles, a North Coast winemaker, as general partners.

The operation began when the Bernsteins bought the ranch, to get away from the bustle of the city. But the area became more and more attractive to them as time went on. The ranch was a prune orchard, and for several years they trained, sprayed, pruned, picked and marketed the crop. There was a log cabin on the property, built by the former owner from material in the land, trees and rocks. It has proved a comfortable home for Mike and Arlene Bernstein, and has undergone only slight renovation during their tenure.

In 1965 they began planting a few grapes in areas not taken up by prunes; this continued through the next two years. By 1968 they began taking out prunes and planted 15 acres to Cabernet Sauvignon, one acre to Merlot. They moved to Mt. Veeder permanently in 1970.

During the years of planting, Mike and Arlene worked with their own hands, preparing the land and cultivating the vines, watering them during hot summers until they were established. By 1970 there was a light crop—"and from then on," says Mike, "the thing just sort of evolved naturally. We saw that this was what we had been looking for—a quality of life that we had not known before."

Kim Giles came into the picture naturally too. They met him during his years at Mayacamas, a neighboring winery and vineyard. As their own vineyard evolved, they visited Mayacamas, talked to Kim about grapes and vineyards, and noted what was being done at Mayacamas. When Kim left to become winemaker at Hanzell in Sonoma County, they kept in touch. In 1970, Kim made the first Mt. Veeder Winery wine, a Cabernet, in the Bernstein's home, followed by a vintage in 1971. The results encouraged all of them to talk about a partnership and winery, which came about in 1972.

Kim Giles learned winemaking under the tutelage of Brad Webb, whose rise to the top of his profession had its roots at Hanzell. Brad became a wine consultant to give more scope to his expertise, and he has lent a guiding hand to many Napa Valley wineries.

The winery design was created by the three, and all work other than actual construction was done by their own hands. Mike is vineyard manager and business head. Kim makes the wine, and Arlene fits in as needed. They are concentrating on Cabernet "with lots of color and character." No wines will be ready for the market before 1976.

The Bernsteins are not alone among valley vintners who have fled the big city scene, but they are probably one of the couples most content with the change in life style.

VEEDERCREST VINEYARDS

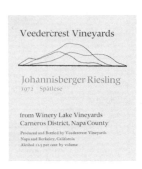

Veedercrest Vineyards

Johannisberger Riesling
1972 Spätlese

from Winery Lake Vineyards
Carneros District, Napa County

Produced and Bottled by Veedercrest Vineyards
Napa and Berkeley, California
Alcohol 12.5 per cent by volume

This winery, with vineyards on Mt. Veeder, west of Napa, has a small pilot plant, geared to 1000 cases per year, in the basement of the winemaker's Berkeley home.

The group of owners includes general partners Alfred W. Baxter, manager and winemaker, and Attorney Ronald Fenolio, in charge of finances. Others involved are Pat Baker, ranch manager, and Craig Hall, head of vineyard operations.

Vineyards are presently being developed on the 300-acre ranch in the Mayacamas Mountains. When the project is complete, in 1980, Veedercrest will have plantings of Chardonnay, White Riesling, and some of each of the major red Bordeaux varieties, such as Cabernet Franc, Merlot, Bouschet, Petite Verdot, Cabarnet Sauvignon and Malbec.

Mt. Veeder is an extinct volcano, and on its slopes the soil is thin and dry, suited to vines and giving them the stress they need to produce grapes with the potential for great wine. In the past few years, the Mt. Veeder area has come into its own as a district for growing superb wine grapes, and, though formerly devoted to second homes for city people, its land is being cleared and planted to grapes by several other vintners. Crops are not bountiful, but possess a quality and character with great regional distinctiveness.

In order to get its label established and its wines on the market, the firm began making wines with grapes from Rene di Rosa's Winery Lake Vineyard in Los Carneros district, and from Ernie van Asperan's vineyard near St. Helena. Production is divided between Chardonnay, White Riesling (Spatlese and Beerenauslese), Cabernet Sauvignon, Merlot and Pinot Noir. Cooperage experiments with Limousin, Nevers, Troncais, Yugoslav and American oak are under way.

Veedercrest's first commercial wine, a 1972 White Riesling, won a bronze medal at the Los Angeles County Fair, and has done well consistently in comparative tastings at San Francisco's Vintners' Club.

Wines are being distributed nationally, even internationally. They are available in Boston, Washington, D. C., and at major wine shops in the Bay Area, Santa Cruz and Carmel. Distribution in Southern California and through restaurants and clubs is planned in the near future. Veedercrest is among the very small circle of California wineries to have its wines in the cellars of Michelin-starred restaurants in France.

Veedercrest has a corporate subsidiary, Mt. Veeder Vineyards, Inc., which is becoming active in wine imports, and as the U. S. representative of small, quality brandy producers in the Bas-Armagnac district of France.

Interestingly, the name Veedercrest came into being after it was discovered by the owners that the name they had plannd to use on their label, Mr. Veeder Vineyards, had already been registered for use in 1938, by Peter Mondavi and Charles Krug. Although Mondavi does not actively use the name, it is still his, and the winery became Veedercrest. The label on the bottle is a design of Jack Staufacher, of San Francisco's Greenwood Press.

MAYACAMAS VINEYARDS

The Mayacamas Winery is reached by a road winding through the wooded mountain country separating Napa and Sonoma Valleys. High on the slopes of Mt. Veeder, an extinct volcano, the winery setting is magnificent, and the view of valley and hills has an untamed grandeur that is unforgettable. Deer, cougar and bobcats are resident in the area; Mayacamas was the name a valley Indian tribe gave to the mountain range and is said to mean "howl of the mountain lion."

The winery is ten miles northwest of Napa, at 1900 feet elevation. John Henry Fisher, a San Francisco pickle merchant, from Stuttgart, built the native stone winery in 1889, and planted the hillside vineyards. His attempt at growing grape varieties such as Zinfandel and "Sweetwater" is captured in "The Vineyard," written by that master wine country writer, Idwal Jones. The story depicts the mountain vine growers of the time with warmth and honesty. They were a breed apart, a hardier lot than those who grew vines on the valley floor. The statement "He who plants a vine becomes entangled in its branches," is never more appropriate than when applied to the old-time mountain vineyardists.

Fisher sold the property at the turn of the century. It was allowed to run down during Prohibition, and was not reclaimed until Jack and Mary Taylor purchased it in 1941. The distillery building became a comfortable home, and the winery, formerly called "Mt. Veeder Vineyards," was renamed Mayacamas.

During the next 20 years, the Taylors replanted the vineyards to Chardonnay and Cabernet Sauvignon at great expense and endless toil. This couple gave the area a legacy of fine wines through their extraordinary foresight and dedication to the vine. They left a mark on the land and on many palates, for their wine had the strength and vigor of mountain grown vines.

By 1961 the management of Mayacamas was left in younger hands. The Taylors, commuting between Napa and New York, began offering stock to their customers at $10 a share. This enabled Mayacamas to double its small capacity, and the Taylors made it available in exclusive restaurants and wine shops, where it won recognition for excellence.

Bob Travers, a Stanford graduate, and six limited partners took control of Mayacamas in 1968. He did not come to the winery as a neophite, as many did in that era. His research over the years included trips to Europe and enology courses at UC Davis. An apprenticeship at Heitz Cellars gave him valuable experience. Now he makes his home in the converted distillery, with his wife and children. In the interest of pursuing excellence he has limited offerings to three wines, hoping, by doing so, to improve the already fine wines traditionally made at Mayacamas. His Late Harvest Zinfandel has been widely acclaimed.

He continues to plant, wrestle with rocky hillside soil, losing one grape stake in three to its resistance. Upholding the precedent of making great wine that began in 1889 is of utmost importance to this dedicated winemaker.

CLOS DU VAL VINEYARDS

This new winery, off Silverado Trail near Chimney Rock Golf Course, at Yountville, is constructed of aggregate and timber, with arched stained glass windows. There is a red concrete tile roof, and the architecture by Keith & Associates of Santa Rosa is reminiscent of old California in the days of George Yount. The setting is at the southeastern end of Napa Valley. The site is rural and scenic, with a backdrop of low foothills covered with spreading oaks, behind these the jagged outcroppings of Stag's Leap. The valley narrows here, bringing the western hills into a feeling of intimacy with the site, and at the rear and sides are the greens of the golf course. Around the winery are the vineyards of Cabernet Sauvignon and Zinfandel grapes, the only two varieties from which the wines will be made.

A young Frenchman, Bernard Portet, is winemaker and manager, and one of the limited partners owning the winery. He came to this country in early 1972, and crushed the first of the winery's Cabernet and Zinfandel that fall. During the first years of its existence, the winery used as its base of operations the old Occidental Winery in a nearby location. This is an interesting structure, built by T. L. Grigsby in 1878, on land that was part of the Yount grant from Mexico. It will continue to be used as a storage facility.

Young Portet, a member of a French winemaking family, is a graduate of Montpelier University with a degree in viticulture, enology and agronomy. He comments that Napa Valley was chosen for the winery "because it has great potential." Of all the wine growing regions of the world he has seen, this seemed the most favorable spot to launch the winery enterprise. "There are very good wines made here, with lots of finesse and character. Besides that, the valley is a good place to live and work—there is a certain ambience here." He speaks English perfectly, with little accent.

The winery building is 150 feet by 90 feet; it is planned that it will be a small winery, with no more than 14,000 or 15,000 cases—30,000 to 40,000 gallons, made each year.

As with several of the other new valley wineries, no visitor facilities are at Clos du Val, and none are planned for the future. "This is a working winery," says Portet. There is not a retail room at the winery, at present, but one is planned. Wines will be marketed through retail stores.

The 1972 Zinfandel and Cabernet Sauvignon were released in the fall of 1974, only two years old, and capable of further development through judicious cellaring. The wines are drinkable, says the winemaker, but can be improved by further aging. It depends on personal preference, he remarks, how much more age is desirable.

Speaking of the future, Portet looks forward to a long life of living and making good wine in Napa Valley, but he remains a true Frenchman—"When I retire, I will probably want to go back to live in France," he says.

STAG'S LEAP WINE CELLARS

Located about a mile north of Chimney Rock on the Silverado Trail, the newly-completed Stag's Leap Wine Cellars nestles at the foot of a wooded knoll. The winery, of redwood and stone, is reached by a road winding up through majestic oaks. A carved redwood sign in the shape of a wine cask carries the name.

The first Cabernet Sauvignon grapes from the home vineyards were crushed in 1972 at a neighboring winery under Stag's Leap Wine Cellars supervision. The new winery was completed in 1973 when Cabernet Sauvignon and Johannisberg Riesling were crushed. Plans call for yearly crushes of 300 to 400 tons of varieties grown in the Stag's Leap Vineyards and certain selected vineyards in the same cool growing region at the south end of the valley. Warren Winiarski, general partner and manager, plans to maintain regional distinctiveness in his wines. He will not blend, but will produce 100% varietal wines, all vintaged, from vineyards usually given label recognition.

Winiarski has spent several years studying the arts and disciplines of winemaking. He spent two years with Lee Stewart at the original Souverain Cellars, followed by two years at the Robert Mondavi Winery. During these and subsequent years of consulting work and vineyard management, he came to choose the site for the future winery's home Cabernet vineyard in what he regards as one of the most favorable locations for this variety in the valley—the Stag's Leap area.

Everyone in the Winiarski family has been involved in the vineyard and winery operations from the beginning. The three children have always had chores suited to their abilities and are learning the wine business from the vineyard ground up. Warren's wife, Barbara, supervises winery art work and public relations and doubles as expert taster for the wines as Warren guides them through the various stages of their development and finishing. It is expected to continue as a small, family-contained operation.

The name of the winery comes from the prominent and impressive landmark visible from the valley floor as a series of escarpments or crags in the eastern foothills. There is even a legendary stag said to be involved in giving the area its name. There was an old hotel nearby in the early part of the century called Stag's Leap Manor. There are plans to establish a winery on this property and there will be two wineries using the Stag's Leap regional name on their labels. This is not an unusual situation in winegrowing sections of Europe, where names and labels are often very similar. The wine drinker learns to observe labels, and discriminates among wines with similar appellations, so that he will always be sure what he is drinking. In such a small area as Napa Valley the use of a regional designation by two neighboring wineries is a reason for reading the label with care—a good practice at any time.

As founders of one of the new wineries in the valley whose history is still to be written, the Winiarski family hopes to be able, during the coming years, to make a place and a name for Stag's Leap Wine Cellars.

STAG'S LEAP WINERY

This fabulous old estate is a part of Napa Valley's historical past. It is now the home of Stag's Leap Winery, not to be confused with Stag's Leap Wine Cellars, just up the road. It is owned by Carl and Joanne Doumani, who left the world of Los Angeles big business in 1970.

The old hotel, now their home, is a picturesque building constructed in 1888 by Horace Chase. It has two stories of cut stone; a third story of wood was pulled down during restoration, and the roofline has been turreted to look like a Medieval fortress. Inside, the rooms are spacious and high ceilinged.

The winery building is of field stone and stands near the house. It was operated as a winery by the Chase family, using the Stag's Leap label of which their present label is a reproduction. The aging cellars and stone-lined caves will be restored by 1975 and will become their winery. Meanwhile, their grapes are being crushed and fermented at a neighboring winery, to their specifications.

The estate, home of Horace and Minnie (Meisner) Chase, was purchased after their deaths by the Fred Grange family, who converted it to a hotel in 1920. During the next decades, it was the "in" spot for the flaming youth of the period to make merry. It is rumored that, in this out-of-the-way spot, bootleg liquor flowed freely, and that the row of small cabins at the rear were occupied by ladies of the night as an added attraction. However, during its heyday some prestigious names graced the register, among them the King and Queen of Portugal.

The hotel closed in 1953, and a period of neglect set in. During its years of vacancy the house was stripped of many of its original fittings; chandeliers, doors and other salable items. The Doumanis found the remains of handsome gardens, which they are gradually conquering and taking back from the wild. The site is on a knoll, and there is a swimming pool, criss-crossed with cracks, which they hope to restore with gunnite. There are wide verandas, beamed redwood ceilings and lovely redwood paneling. A couple who occupied the field-stone carriage house from 1953 to 1970, Joseph and Rose Willis, recently wrote a book about Stag's Leap Ranch, called "Biography of a Manor House," recalling the grandeur of the Chase regime.

Stag's Leap Winery is a limited partnership. The Doumanis are the general partners and they have four limited partners: Peter Simon, Lionel Banks, Bob Christen and Joe McNeil.

The planned output at Stags Leap Winery is 10,-000 cases annually, a small operation devoted to making wine from their own 100 acre vineyard, which is gradually being replanted in Chenin Blanc, Petite Sirah, Cabernet Sauvignon and Pinot Noir.

The Herculean labor of restoring the buildings and grounds looms ahead of the Doumanis, but they are confident that it is within their capabilities, and look forward to the time when Stag's Leap Winery will assume its rightful place among valley wineries.

OAKVILLE VINEYARDS

This winery formerly belonged to Bartolucci Brothers, along with 296 acres of varietal grapes. It operated under various names until its sale to Oakville Vineyards in 1969.

Heading Oakville Vineyards is Wilfred (Bud) van Loben Sels, the general partner in a limited partnership involving 383 other investors. The van Loben Sels, Bud and Jean, became acquainted with Peter Becker during his years as winemaker at Almaden Vineyards in Santa Clara County. The three decided they wanted to work together as a team, and began a search for a suitable functioning winery for their enterprise. The search ended at Bartolucci Vineyards.

The scheme to finance via the route of a limited partnership resulted in enough capital to launch the operation, and the winery was opened, with a tasting room, gift shop, picnic area and an array of gay banners waving to beckon the public to its location, well back from the highway at Oakville Cross Road.

Bud van Loben Sels is a native Californian. His father was manager of Stanford lands, including the winery, for the university. After graduating from University of California at Berkeley, Bud took up residence at Carmel. Visits to Almaden Winery, then under Louis Benoist, resulted in his friendship with Becker.

Peter Karl Becker, Oakville winemaster, was born in Germany, where he studied biology and chemistry and had a small winery. He came to the USA in 1955, and his work with Almaden saw its development from a relatively small operation to a large one. Becker's winemaking theories include the use of centrifuges, and eschews the use of oak in aging white wines.

Oakville Associates purchased the Captain Gustave Niebaum home from the Daniels Estate when it came on the market in 1972. Bud and Jean van Loben Sels rejuvenated the house and grounds, and made it their residence. "It really belongs to everybody who loves wine and wine history," says Jean, "so we try to share it as much as we can." Associates and partners are free to visit and enjoy the luxury and magnificense of the mansion, formerly owned by Inglenook.

The sale included 120 acres of the famous Inglenook Ranch, which produced some of the grapes on which the Inglenook reputation was founded. Limited partners with vineyards give Oakville control of about 600 more acres of Napa Valley vineyard. In addition, the estate includes 1500 acres of woodland and landscaped lawns and gardens.

With more than 1000 acres of vineyard producing grapes for Oakville Vineyards, Becker has succeeded in creating a tradition with the Oakville "Our House" wines—a white, a red and a rose—made to sell at an extremely moderate price. A line of fine premium varietals are marketed under the Oakville and van Loben Sels labels.

The winery and its vineyards were launched at the beginning of the wine boom, and its production of 40,000 cases annually is expected to reach 100,000 cases by 1978.

ROBERT MONDAVI WINERY

This winery, just north of Oakville on Highway 29, is a perfect example of maintaining old family tradition and wedding it to the best of the new. It was founded by Robert Mondavi, of C. Mondavi & Sons at Charles Krug, after what is described by Leon Adams as "a family tiff." Leaving his younger brother Peter in charge of Charles Krug Winery, Bob left the family firm in 1966 to begin construction on his own. Mondavi shares ownership in the enterprise with Sick's Ranier Brewing Company of Seattle.

The handsome Mission-style winery, designed by Architect Cliff May, is set back among vineyards, with long corridors, Spanish tile floors and dark wood paneling, and is dedicated to hospitality and community involvement. In this setting, Robert and his elder son Michael make up a father-and-son team which has been advantageous to both. They have established their own label and gained it a position of respect in the valley.

Although it is a large winery, one million plus gallons fermenting capacity, and has experienced several building expansions since it was founded, every effort is made to give it an aura of friendliness and informality. The Mondavi approach to wine tours and tastings involves the handling of visitors in small groups, having several small tasting rooms, and giving visitors a pleasing feeling of stature and importance. The retail sales room plays down the commercial aspect, while selling visitors

one-tenth of the winery's considerable output. Public Relations Director Margrit Biever speaks eight languages, including Japanese, and charms visitors by addressing them in their own tongue.

The winery is supplied with grapes by some 800 acres of varietal vineyards in the Oakville-Yountville area. Each piece of equipment purchased is of the finest and most modern design and manufacture, with jacketed stainless steel tanks, small European oak cooperage, and a well-equipped laboratory for its staff of enologists. The Mondavis, father and son, have combed Europe and the USA to gather together the best of equipment and technique, which is constantly being re-evaluated.

Robert Mondavi is a dynamic, slightly graying man with 38 years' experience in winemaking since his graduation from Stanford in 1936.

Bob Mondavi has to his credit many years of community service; as past president and director of Napa Valley Vintner's Association, a founder and director of Napa Valley Wine Technical Association, and as a member and former board chairman of Wine Institute. His is total involvement—if he takes a trip, it is a "busman's holiday" to visit, view and learn from other wineries in other places.

Early in his involvement with wine, Bob realized that the trend away from bulk wines to fine table wines was the direction of the future. With this in mind, he traveled extensively during the next two decades. On the East coast, he found that the image of California wines desperately needed upgrading. Whatever their merit, the wines had not achieved acceptance in the best restaurants and retail shops. Bob Mondavi threw him-

The inner courtyard at Mondavi.

self into an intensive campaign to find the reason behind this lack of prestige, and bent his considerable energies toward changing the picture.

He spent the years from 1943 to 1960 in traveling, studying, selecting, buying, tasting, evaluating and comparing California wines with those acclaimed as the world's best. Several times each year he traveled to Eastern and Mid-Western cities, an ambassador for California wines. The industry owes him a debt of gratitude for his unflagging diligence in pursuing this goal until, in the 1960's, it was finally achieved, and California wines, particularly Napa Valley wines, were accorded their place in the sun.

If no man is a hero to his valet, he is usually less so to his immediate family. However, his son Michael is one of Bob's most sincere admirers. Mike came into the business during his college years, starting at the bottom, given no special consideration because he was the son of the boss. Bob insisted that his son learn every phase of the business from the ground up. "My first job was in sanitation," remembers Mike. "That's a fancy name for scrubbing barrels." Now head of production and sales at the winery, he is well versed in every detail of the operation, and his thorough grounding has served him well.

A younger son, Tim, soon to complete his studies in enology at UC Davis, will join the family firm, where he has been working during summer vacations. He has learned all phases of the winemaking business, according to his father's theories of winery procedures.

The Robert Mondavi theories of winemaking include a firm belief in aging in wood to bring out the character and complexities of the wines. "The kiss of wood" is of vital importance, they believe, and a touch of oak is evident in all Robert Mondavi wines.

Mike believes that climate, soil, grape variety, facilities, knowledge and know-how, plus desire and will, make an unbeatable combination in producing fine wine. Of these, he believes, climate is the most important, and the climate of Napa Valley the greatest asset the Mondavi wines can claim. However, desire and will are among the strongest elements the Mondavi team has brought to the endeavor.

The wines produced have won recognition from upper echelon wine people. Eleven leading winemakers in California sampled their own Cabernet Sauvignon at a blind tasting in September, 1972. The wine writer-lecturer Robert Balzer conducted the tasting and found Robert Mondavi's 1969 Cabernet Sauvignon to be the winner.

The Vineyard Room, a large facility at the rear of the complex, opening on wide green lawns, has a rotating display of prominent Napa Valley and California artists. It is the setting for many community events. Twice a year a concert series is held; in summer, the stage and seating are set up on the lawns; in winter, musical events are held in the Vineyard Room, with a cheery fire blazing on the hearth and wine tasting during intermission.

The Robert Mondavi wines include Chardonnay, Pinot Noir, Gamay, Chenin Blanc, Riesling, Johannisberg Riesling, Traminer, Cabernet Sauvignon and Gamay Rose. A dessert wine, Moscato d'Oro, has been added to the line. All are vintage dated.

INGLENOOK VINEYARDS

Captain Gustave Niebaum could have built his winery anywhere in the world. He chose Napa Valley, purchasing the property south of Rutherford in 1880. At the time he bought the estate it was a sanitarium, celebrated for its mineral springs and health-giving climate.

Gustave Ferdinand Nybom (later Niebaum) was born in 1842 under Russian rule in Helsinki, Finland. He went to sea as a boy, and through diligent enterprise, sailed a ship to Alaska under his own command in 1864. By 1867 he had become so proficient at bartering for furs and acquainting himself with the region that he became a partner in the Alaska Commercial Company, which paid the U. S. government more for the exclusive fur sealing rights than the government paid for the entire Alaska purchase.

Having accumulated a fortune, he bought the 1000-acre estate known as Inglenook, a Scottish expression meaning "cosy corner" or "fireside." Niebaum was determined to make Inglenook the most celebrated winery in California. He imported cuttings from the finest vineyards in Europe, planting them with care and regard for maintaining and enhancing the beauty of nature. Along with the fine oak cooperage he imported from Germany, he also procured an unprecedented and extremely valuable library of books dealing with wine.

To give his wines a proper home, Captain Niebaum erected the cellar and winery, completed in 1887. It was said to have no equal, for perfection of detail and elegant finish, anywhere in America. The architecture is semi-Gothic. The stone and iron structure, with its arched vaults, was a model of efficiency and cleanliness, and the Captain held his crew to a high standard in all winery operations.

Frona Eunice Wait, writing in 1889, says: "'Mould, cobwebs and dust, did you say?' remarked the genial manager, Mr. John Armstrong, upon a recent visit to Inglenook. 'I assure you, Madam, that if Captain Niebaum should discover either . . . in any of the nooks and crannies, I should be obliged to pack my traps and get, despite the fact that I have been in his service for 20 years. Cleanliness is our watchword.'"

Mrs. Wait described Inglenook as the California equivalent of Schloss Johannisberg in Germany, or Chateau Lafite in France. In 1889 the captain achieved his goal—the Inglenook wines won quality awards for overall excellence at the Paris Exposition. They continued to do so until his death in 1908.

Captain Neibaum had a penchant for success, his life history attests to his business prowess. Much like our present day Howard Hughes, outside of his close circle of prestigious friends, he was virtually unknown to the general public. He never granted a personal interview and it appears that his many days at sea fostered the solitary habits he developed on land. Nevertheless he established an elegant winery for elegant wines which still stands as a tribute to the colorful seafarer.

The tradition of making fine vintages for love of creating superlative wine, seldom showing a profit but winning acclaim in this country and abroad, continued

Cask aging wines at Inglenook.

after the death of Niebaum. Prohibition closed the winery in 1919, but Repeal in 1933 saw it reopened, its former glory restored and its integrity intact. The Captain's widow intrusted to Carl Bundschu, of the prestigious pre-Prohibition winemaking firm of Gundlach & Bundschu, the responsibility of maintaining the reputation of the winery in its days of glory. Later this responsibility was shared with John Daniel, a grandnephew of Mrs. Neibaum, and under their direction Inglenook maintained its position of prominence by allowing, as did Capt. Niebaum, only the finest bottles to be marketed.

At Inglenook it is tempting to dwell on the romance of the past but the modern era dawned in 1964 when Daniel surprised the industry and the wine community by selling Inglenook to United Vintners, thus bringing a great family tradition to an end. He remained with the winery until his death in 1970. His impact on the wine industry and his dedication to producing prestige varietal wines, without compromise, has made him immortal.

When Inglenook, under new ownership, began expansion, plans were formulated with the preservation of the historic site and bearing vineyards in mind. The picturesque winery, which has enchanted Napa Valley visitors for nearly 100 years, will become one of a complex of four buildings. The new construction includes a monolithic barrel aging cellar directly in front of the old winery. When the complex is completed, there will be a view of the winery framed by an archway at the end of the long access drive. There is to be a courtyard, with trees, flowers and fountains, in the square formed by the buildings.

This expansion places the winery in a three million plus gallon capacity category. The vineyard holdings have been enlarged to include 1500 additional valley acres formerly owned by members of Allied Grape Growers Cooperative, of which United Vintners is the marketing arm. Heublein Inc. bought United Vintners in 1968.

The same estate bottled, vintage dated varietals are still being made, as are the special "cask selection" vintages of some of Inglenook's most prestigious wines. Included is the famous Charbono, brought to the Napa Valley as early as 1861 from the Piedmont region in Italy, which resembles Barbera. The line has been expanded to include generic and "district" wines which are sold under the "Inglenook Vintage" label for less than the estate bottled wines, and the less expensive Navalle wines. Other additions include the Champagne and dessert wines.

Tours and tastings have been instituted under the new ownership. One of the sights is the Captain Niebaum sampling room, an exquisite gem furnished with pieces that would do credit to a museum. The interior, with its richly carved chairs, elaborate sideboard, large table with crystal drinking cups, all lit by the soft glow of light through stained glass windows, are as they were in the time of the Captain. Leon D. Adams calls it "a gustatory chapel."

The winemaker, Tom Ferrell, is one of the new breed of enologists turned out by the School of Enology at Davis. Inglenook places great hopes on his efforts in the future.

BEAULIEU VINEYARDS

The Beaulieu Vineyards at Rutherford has enjoyed a position of immense prestige among Napa Valley wineries for three-quarters of a century.

The winery was founded at the turn of the century by Georges de Latour, a young Frenchman of no particular wealth, who arrived in California some 15 years earlier with wine on his mind. He began traveling the North Coast wine country, buying sediment and crust from wine tanks for making baking powder. But he was planning for the day when he would be a winegrower and winemaker.

Finally he had amassed enough capital to buy a wheat farm on the outskirts of Rutherford. The estate was named Beaulieu, "beautiful place" by his wife. He journeyed to France to bring back the finest cuttings for his vineyard, and opened a small winery. Later he acquired additional vineyards at Oakville and the Carneros District, a total of 745 acres of prime wine-growing land planted to the best varietal grapes. He would tolerate nothing second rate—where his winery was concerned, everything must be of the finest.

Some years later he bought the Seneca Ewer winery, a small building across the highway from his home vineyard, enlarging it and making it the main cellar, thus correcting the winery's only fault, lack of space, and allowing more than one half million fifths to mature in glass before shipment to wine-lovers.

When others were forced to close down during Prohibition, de Latour's business flourished, for he built up a nation-wide market in altar wines. At Repeal, he was one of the fortunate few with well-aged wines to release.

Georges and Fernande de Latour enlarged their Victorian home, which stands at the end of a mile-long avenue of flowing plum trees with white-washed trunks, amid beautiful lawns and formal gardens. They spared no expense or effort to make Beaulieu all its name implied, the most beautiful place in the valley. The setting is a valley landmark, which is depicted on the Beaulieu label.

The de Latours were gracious hosts, and entertained many of the great of their day—presidents, ministers, ambassadors and visiting nobility. Madame de Latour, the great lady of California viticulture, was famous for her generosity. When Masson Winery burned down in 1941, she came forward with an offer of red wines although the Beaulieu supply was sparse for public demand. They traveled to France every year, and this resulted in the marriage of their daughter Helene to the Marquis de Pins.

Fernande de Latour was a grande dame of the old school; Georges a cultivated country gentleman who traveled, mingled with the great, and knew wines and the men who made them. When he had to employ a new winemaker, in 1937, he went to France with his son-in-law, seeking the right man. He found Andre Tchelistcheff, a young Russian research scientist working at the winery at the Institit National Agronomique in Paris. He brought him to Napa Valley, a fact on

Vineyards seen from Beaulieu Champagne Cellars.

which he had occasion to congratulate himself. The young Tchelistcheff, in his early 30's, was fired with ambition to make fine wine, and had the flair to do it. He came with the latest French enological and viticulture research at his fingertips.

When the new enologist first tasted the valley wines, he decided that the Cabernet Sauvignon grown here was destined for greatness. For years he urged de Latour to concentrate on making only Cabernet Sauvignon, or at most one or two other wines, but this was not considered feasable at the time. He influenced de Latour to build a special cellar, aging the wine in small oak cooperage, then in the bottle, for a total of four years. The resulting wine was a sensation; Cabernet is still one of the wines for which Beaulieu is famous, and there has never been enough to satisfy the demand.

Tschelistcheff's work at Beaulieu, his influence on the image of Napa Valley wine, has probably not been equalled by any other figure in the wine world today. He made wines in the great European tradition, watching over vineyards and grapes with great devotion, harvesting at exactly the right moment. He has an uncanny ability to judge and evaluate grapes and wine, and to give each the treatment to bring out its optimum qualities. He served as consultant to other wineries, tutored many young enologists, encouraged other wine men to establish themselves in the valley.

Georges de Latour died in 1940. His wife succeeded him as head of Beaulieu until her death in 1951, when it came into possession of their daughter, Marquise de Pins.

In 1969 a family tradition came to an end when the historic winery, whose name was synonymous with the finest vintages, was sold to Heublein Inc. The estate, with its gardens, its avenue of flowering plum, together with a small vineyard and the original winery, remain in the family. The original winery is leased by Hublein as a champagne making facility.

Under Heubelin, limited expansion is the order of the day. New facilities enable Beaulieu to handle up to a 4,000-ton crush. Adjoining land was bought, and a 250,000 case warehouse constructed. Total annual production is 180,000 cases, and a modest increase is planned for future vintages. Wines are fermented in open tanks of stainless steel, and removed to aging cellar cooperage by a network of fibreglass lines. Current cellarmaster is Theo Rosenbrand; enologist is Thomas Selfridge. Another staff member, Maynard Monaghan, is completing twenty years of service at Beaulieu, giving a feeling of continuity to the enterprise. Three generations of the Tchelistcheff family have seen service at the winery; Andre's son Dmitri is technical director, and his grandson, Paul, is an apprentice in Champagne production.

The new owners emphasize that Beaulieu Vineyards has retained its identity through the change of ownership and that the traditions of Georges de Latour are not dead.

The visitor center at Rutherford Square is new, created to accomodate a large number of guests. There are gardens, fountains, art works, a tasting room and a theatre, where films on wine and winemaking are shown. All is done to lend emphasis to the concept that Beaulieu is the star in Heublein's crown.

CAYMUS VINEYARDS

Caymus Vineyards is a project of Charles Wagner, an oldtime grower who became interested in making wine as a hobby, and eventually went commercial, in a limited way.

The winery, located at 8700 Conn Creek Road, Rutherford, was built by Charles and Lorna Wagner on the rear of their property in 1972. The ranch itself has an interesting history. Wagner purchased it in 1941 from Minnie Freyermuth, a daughter of pioneer Napa Valleyan Henry H. Harris, a grower and winemaker of the 1800's. Harris had bought the property from George Yount, the holder of the Mexican grant Rancho Caymus. The name "Caymus" is said to be that of the tribe of Indians living on the land at the time George Yount came to the valley in 1843.

Also on the Freyermuth property is the original H. H. Harris Winery, a picturesque stone building which was purchased by the Douglas Pringles (who later owned Schramsberg for a few years), in 1940. Pringle converted it into a handsome mansion which was their home. Mrs. Pringle's son by a former marriage, Jose Cebrian, presently resides in the old winery-turned-mansion. It was unfortunately gutted by fire in 1972, and is now being restored to its former state by its owners.

The Wagners erected a utility-type building to serve as their first winery, and this facility is being augmented by another building adjacent to the first, to house bottle storage. Wagner has added 5,000 gallon stainless steel tanks to his wood fermenting tanks, and a small cooperage for aging.

Wines made include Pinot Noir, Pinot Noir Blanc, Cabernet Sauvignon and Johannisberg Riesling. To these, Wagner is adding a Zinfandel, made from grapes purchased in Sonoma County, in the Dry Creek area, in Amador County and from the Lodi area. He is making, blending and aging a Zinfandel which he believes will be unlike any other on the market. It should prove complex and characterful, he says. He is uncertain when it will be released—"not until it is ready," he adds.

The Wagner vineyards are a model of good vineyard housekeeping. They are clean and well cared for, bearing out the idea that good wine depends on good grapes grown by correct vineyard techniques and with that something extra that loving care can provide. Wagner tends his grapes carefully, thinning them judiciously so the vines will not bear more fruit than they can mature successfully. There are about 70 acres in his home vinyard. With the exception of his Zinfandel mentioned above, all his wines are estate bottled.

He does not envision that this winery will ever be any larger than its present capacity, which is between 20,000 and 25,000 gallons. Wines are distributed through local retail outlets, and may also be bought at the winery in case lots.

There are no formal visitor facilities at Caymus, but interested friends of wine are welcomed by Charles and Lorna Wagner, and may view the premises, the winery buildings, the vineyards, and taste available wine.

SOUVERAIN CELLARS

This winery was founded in 1943 by J. Leland Stewart, a retired advertising man who started it as virtually a hobby, then became deeply involved in producing fine wine. He was able to achieve some excellent vintages, and soon won the acclaim of wine lovers. His wines received many awards over the years.

Stewart's wines were made from the classic French and German grape varieties. He learned as he went; as he said: "I am not one of those with wine in my blood." A great deal of winemaking is plain hard work, he said, and went on working to improve his wines, making them known to connoisseurs over the state. He was the first vintner to introduce a varietal Green Hungarian wine, very dry and flavorful, which soon induced a host of imitators.

What had been intended as a retirement avocation assumed such proportions that Stewart began thinking about expansion possibilities. He became involved with new partners, they sold the Howell Mountain winery and relocated Souverain Cellars just off Silverado Trail east of Rutherford. The hillside setting is studded with giant oaks, and blooms with flowers in the spring.

Stewart's partners include the minority interest owned by individual investors; and Pillsbury Company, the well-known food chain, which holds the majority interest.

The new winery is designed in the architectural style of an old-time Napa Valley barn, and is the work of John Marsh Davis, of Marin County. The warmth of wood is emphasized in construction of the building, which is both spacious and functional, with exposed beams lending an atmosphere of strength and solidarity.

The winery has been equipped with completely modern automated crushing and fermenting facilities, of stainless steel, and there are large aging and storage rooms in the airy, high-ceilinged building. With it all Souverain does not envision ever being a large winery, but holding production to about 75,000 cases annually.

Another policy is the national distribution of Souverain Cellars wines. It is felt that, although the demand in California would take the entire production, the wines should be more widely known and appreciated.

To further these plans and desires, it was decided to concentrate the entire effort on eight varietals—those which had established the Souverain reputation in the first place. These are four reds: Cabernet Sauvignon, Pinot Noir, Zinfandel and Petite Sirah; and four whites: Chardonnay, Johannisberg Riesling, Green Hungarian and Pineau Souverain. There is also the distinctive Los Amigos Sherry Sack, a Stewart specialty.

Souverain purchases its grapes from independent valley growers. Baxter is concerned with selecting only the choicest grapes of each variety, from wherever they may be found in Napa Valley, as a continuation of Stewart's policies. The advantage of this method, says Baxter, is that it allows the winemaker to carefully choose and select the grapes for each year's crush, rejecting any that are not up to their standards of quality.

Lee Stewart remains a Souverain advisor.

CHAPPELLET VINEYARDS

CHAPPELLET
VINEYARD
1971
Napa Valley
CABERNET SAUVIGNON

GROWN AND BOTTLED BY CHAPPELLET VINEYARD
PRITCHARD HILL, ST. HELENA, CALIFORNIA.   ALCOHOL 12% BY VOLUME

Among the array of men who have fled the big business scene to make wine in Napa Valley, none is more colorful than Donn Chappellet. His winery is equally dramatic, a pyramid set into a hill in an off-the-beaten-track spot called Pritchard Hill.

The pyramid is huge, 212 feet on each side at the base, with a towering roof of rust-red steel parted by long panels of glass admitting light. At the apex is a room with one of the most breath-taking views in the valley. Far below is the blue jewel of Hennessey Lake, surrounded by hills with forests of oak, madrone and fir, and 100 acres of hillside vineyard planted to noble vines.

Donn tells of leaving the Los Angeles area and his business in the food vending industry, which had unexpectedly burgeoned to bigness. "I started out with another fellow; we never planned to be big, but pretty soon we were involved with thousands of people and thousands of headaches." He parted from this multimillion dollar business with no tears, and began the search for the ideal location to build his winery. Months of scanning and screening brought him to Pritchard Hill in 1967.

Seven years and a great deal of Donn Chappellet have gone into the creation of the vineyards, the winery and the wines, which have received wide acclaim for their excellence. He expects to have the operation firmly in the black in the forseeable future, while keeping the operation small—not exceeding a 60,000 gallon capacity. Chappellet wines, originally made from their own grapes, will soon be receiving grapes from three neighbors. Donn will farm two of the ranches, with the third being operated by a retired neighbor under his direction. This will moderately expand the present production which is marketed to a select mailing list and gone almost as soon as it is announced. Donn has added scope to his wines through distribution to make them known to a wider audience and has developed markets in over twenty states at top restaurants and wine shops.

The winery was three years in the building and is a tribute to function and design. The interior is as interesting and spectacular as it is outside. It consists of one huge room, with a small office at the front. Presses, fermenters, aging cooperage, bottling and packing facilities each occupy an assigned area. The mellowness of wood, the light filtering through glass panels, the lofty apex of the pyramid stretching above, give the same feeling of awe as a grove of mighty redwoods. Along one side are stacked the small oak barrels, where precious wines sleep and ripen until they are judged ready for the bottle.

Above the winery is the long, rambling house where Donn lives with his wife Molly and their six exuberant children. The family has blended gracefully into the life of the valley wine community.

"I wanted to be a winemaker because I knew and liked wine. I wanted to do something that would be a real challenge—that would take everything I could bring to it." Thus Donn Chappellet. He has found the reality as fulfilling as its·promise.

NICHELINI VINEYARDS

James Nichelini is the third generation of a wine-making family in the old Italian tradition. The winery was founded in 1890 by Antone Nichelini, his grandfather, who came from Switzerland near the Italian border and homesteaded the tract of land in 1884. It is eleven miles east of Rutherford on Highway 128, and is a part of the John B. Chiles grant from General Vallejo, made in 1860.

Young Antone was poor but hardworking and determined. In 1890 he built the winery with native stone held together with sand and lime, money to buy cement being lacking. The building is still strong and sound. Atop the two stone stories is a frame house where Antone and his wife Marie raised twelve children.

He planted a vineyard and made wine; his customers were miners from the many magnesium mines in Pope and Chiles Valley, where 200 Italian immigrants lived and toiled. Wages in those days included a ration of wine, and it was Nichelini wine. Mama Marie helped out by baking crisp Italian bread in outdoor ovens for hungry customers to eat while drinking their wine.

Wineries closed during Prohibition, but Antone saw no reason why he should not make an honest living, making and selling his wine as usual. He was finally arrested and had to close down; after Repeal his son came into the business as licensee. The younger Nichelini's interests were never in winemaking, and his son Jim took

over in 1947, becoming a partner in the winery operation with his grandfather.

Nichelini's has a crush of about 15,000 gallons, a one-man operation with extra help during the crush. The owner believes in a simple philosophy of winemaking—a continual move forward to better grapes, better methods, better wines. He has no desire to be bigger; winegrowing and winemaking are a way of life he has found satisfying, and the increased pressures of modern business hold no attraction for him.

Visitors are welcome at Nichelini's, and they will find much to please and interest them in meeting the proprietor and viewing an old-time Italian-Swiss winery that is truly unique. The equipment in use is the same installed nearly 100 years ago, when the winery was built, except now it is motorized. Customers may sit and sip the wines on a deck adjoining the cellar, and if he is not too busy and is in good form, Jim may play the accordion for them.

Nichelini specialties are Chenin Blanc and Sauvignon Vert, but he also makes Zinfandel, Petite Sirah, Napa Gamay and Cabernet Sauvignon. The climate of Chiles Valley, at 900 feet elevation, has become interesting to other vintners, and more vineyards are presently being planted there. The Louis Martini Winery has planted extensive acreage north of Nichelini's, finding it to be a "low Region II." The wines of this area have a discernibly different and interesting local character.

No change seems imminent at Nichelini's, and Jim is hopeful that his son, recently returned from a stint in the armed services, will make the winery a career.

JOSEPH PHELPS VINEYARDS

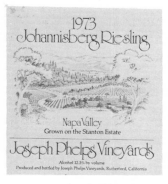

This is a new winery under enthusiastic ownership, with its first wine released in the fall of 1974. The building, at 200 Taplin Road, St. Helena, is of redwood, with heavy timbering and wide overhang. The multi-level structure, with vertical siding and a cedar shingle roof, is architecturally reminiscent of an early California barn.

Its 17,000 square feet are divided into two wings, with an open area in the center, spanned by offices and administrative facilities, which tie the two wings together. The effect is pleasing, blending into surrounding foothills and vineyards.

Such care has been taken to preserve the environment that only one oak tree was removed. Some replanting is under way in sections where trees were cut for grazing by the former owners, Conolly Hereford Ranch. When the 600 acres of rolling hills were deer fenced, it was found that a small herd of deer were enclosed within its confines.

An overhead sprinkler system furnishes frost protection, and water is provided by a dam engineered to rise in a gentle slope, planted with vines to the lip of the lake, making a pleasant view of water, trees and vineyards from the winery. The Spring Valley schoolhouse, green and white with a cupola on top, a familiar Napa Valley landmark, is on the property, and will be carefully preserved, says Joseph Phelps.

The vineyard is planted to Gewurztraminer and Johannisberg Riesling, with reds led by Cabernet Sauvignon and Zinfandel. These, with Chardonnay and Sauvignon Blanc, will comprise the wines made here. There will be about 40,000 cases annually, from their own vineyards as soon as they are bearing. Where other grapes are used, the grower will usually be given credit on the label.

Winemaker-ranch manager Walter Schug, a graduate of the viticulture and enology school in Geisenheim, Germany, came to the USA in 1961. He was trained in Germany, working for major premium wineries of the Rhine area. After coming to the Napa Valley, he served as North Coast representative for E. & J. Gallo, in charge of grower relations and quality control. He is assisted by Bruce Roberts, for several years associated with Stony Hill.

The winery's right wing houses processing, with a bottling and aging section on the left. Offices, kitchen and laboratory are at mezzanine level. Equipment is of the finest design and manufacture, and there are many innovative ideas in practice, to insure high product quality and efficient use of time and manpower. Fermenting and holding capacity adequate for a full vintage is provided by jacketed stainless steel tanks.

German fiberglass tanks provide breakdown storage, with 3000-gallon Slavian oak tanks for aging of the wines. Oak ovals from Germany will be hand carved with vineyard scenes. Small cooperage of French and American oak are individually stored on steel racks for efficient removal and cleaning.

HEITZ WINE CELLARS

VINTAGE 1969   BOTTLED SEPTEMBER, 1973
Bottle No. 12196 of a total of 12,200 bottles

Heitz Cellar

NAPA VALLEY
CABERNET SAUVIGNON
PRODUCED AND BOTTLED IN OUR CELLAR BY
HEITZ WINE CELLARS
ST. HELENA, CALIFORNIA

Joe Heitz has lived in California for three decades, coming first in 1944 after being stationed there during his service in the Air Force. He enrolled at Davis, and graduated with a Master's degree in viticulture and enology.

For the next decade he worked at various leading wineries, including some years at Beaulieu with Andre Tchelistcheff. He later taught viticulture and enology at Fresno State College.

In 1961, Joe and his wife Alice decided they were ready to begin their own winery. They bought the Leon Brendel "Only One" Grignolino winery south of St. Helena, along with 8 acres of Grignolino grapes. Joe still makes Grignolino, said to be the best in California.

The next years were a time of hard work, building up their winery and their label. They had great confidence in their own ability to taste and judge wines, and they selected, blended, matured, bottled and sold wines under the Heitz label. Joe had acquired a reputation for sincerity and integrity; growers with exceptional grapes liked to sell them to him, for they knew they would be handled with respect and expertise. His reputation among connoisseurs sprang up almost at once, and has continued. Alice began assembling a mailing list to be notified as wines were available.

In 1964, Joe and Alice acquired another winery and vineyard, Spring Valley Ranch, at the end of Taplin Road. It had a picturesque old winery of native cut stone, built in 1898, and Heitz equipped it with the best of winemaking machinery and cooperage—a Willmes press, stainless steel fermenters, small Limousin oak cooperage. The ranch has 160 cares of rocks, hills and old vines. Joe planted 20 acres of Grignolino grapes and expects to plant an additional 40 to 50 acres of grapes in the near future.

It is not Joe's intention to dilute his talents as a winemaker with large holdings of vines. He has developed over the years a "solid source of fine grapes from reliable growers", and this asset has helped develop the present day reputation of Heitz Cellars. Grapes from the prestigious growers have the vineyard origin printed on the label and each bottle is numbered as it is labeled.

Alice works along with her husband, while making a family home of the old farmhouse. They make a great team. She is a famous cook and he is a famous winemaker. Wine writer William Massee comments, "Joe is a superb winemaker with an exceptionally keen palate, only seen once or twice in a generation." Joe is always ready to share his knowledge with others. He has trained many young winemakers now making their own reputations. Bob Travers of Mayacamas and Mike Golick of Chateau Montelena are two men who worked with Heitz.

A new winery of cement block and timbers was built in 1972 for aging red wines, storage and offices. The original winery off Highway 29 is the Heitz Cellars tasting and sales room. The eldest Heitz son, David, a recent graduate of Fresno State University, is involved in the family winery and vineyard operation.

SUTTER HOME WINERY

Sutter Home Winery was founded in 1874 by a Swiss winemaker, John Thomann. Later, in 1900, John Sutter and his brother Jacob purchased the winery and changed its name to the present title. (John Sutter is not the Sutter of Sutter's Fort, but a cousin.)

In 1946 it was purchased by the Trinchero family, John and Mario. Present owners are Mario and Mary Trinchero and their two sons, Louis (Bob) and Roger.

Under the Trincheros, the business was operated for many years as a bulk winery, making and selling wine to customers who came to the winery with their jugs to be filled. Their product was well known and popular with the Italian community, and provided them with a good living.

However, since the wine explosion in the valley, and with younger members of the family exerting their influence on policy, it was decided that they needed a specialty—some particular wine or wines that would set them apart. They came upon a Zinfandel vineyard in the Shenandoah Valley in Amador County, and from its grapes made a smallish amount of wine that proved interesting to wine palates.

Encouraged by this success, they made more the next year, and more each succeeding year until now 85 percent of the wine made at Sutter Home is Zinfandel. The balance is their line of dessert and aperitif wines. These bottlings include a Chinato, a sweet and and a dry Vermouth, and a Moscato Amabile.

The operation has expanded; in the past year it has increased production by 80,000 gallons, bringing the winery up to a 170,000 capacity. They have installed an automatic bottling line, and their wines now have national distribution. The Zinfandel and Zinfandel Rose have always been in short supply, inadequate to meet the demand for this exceptional wine.

This is truly a family winery—members of the family do all the chores, with Bob making the wine, Roger handling sales, Mario and Mary working half day at the winery, and a daughter and daughter-in-law handling tasting room, retail sales and secretarial work. They often laugh about selling good red wine, aged four or five years, for $2 a gallon, in the old, pre-wine-bust days. The present day wine, including the vintaged Zinfandel, is moderately priced for today's market. It is an unusually heavy, robust wine, well balanced, with an excellent raspberry nose. There is some tannin, which allows further aging in the purchaser's callar.

The Trincheros of Napa Valley are from a wine-making background in Asti, Northern Italy. They have no vineyards of their own, purchasing all their grapes to provide the annual sale of 25,000 cases. As with many other valley wineries, they have steadfastly refused all offers to sell. Younger members of the family, grandsons of Mario and Mary, are looking toward involvement in the family winery in the future.

There is no formal hospitality center, but visitors are welcomed, and there is always one of the family on hand to offer tasting and wine talk to interested patrons.

LOUIS MARTINI WINERY

This winery was founded by Louis M. Martini, who died in 1974 at the age of 87, but lived long enough to become a legend in his own time. He was of the old school, lent infinite color and drama to the industry image, and made very fine wines over the years.

The winery, at the southern boundary of St. Helena, was built by Louis himself in 1933. It is a concrete and hollow tile insulated cellar where, for many years, visitors tasted the wines at a long counter adjacent to barrels of wine in the storage cellar, the pleasant odor of sleeping vintages in their nostrils. In recent years an addition on the north side of the building was constructed, housing a handsome tasting room and executive offices.

Louis Michael Martini was born in Genoa on the Italian Riviera in 1887. He came to America at age 13 to join his father in the fish business in pre-earthquake San Francisco. The two fishermen dreamed of making wine some day, and in 1906 started a backyard winery. They were dismayed to find the entire vintage spoiled and undrinkable. So young Louis was sent to Italy to learn how to make good wine, entering the Alba School of Enology. So great were his zeal and capacity to learn that he finished the course in one year, returning home to turn out a vintage that satisfied both father and son. The wine was marketed door to door in the Italian community of North Beach.

As time went on Louis became involved with winemaking in various parts of the state. During Prohibition he established a winery in Kingsburg where he made and distributed a grape concentrate for home use, appropriately called "Forbidden Fruit." He had faith that such an unnatural law could not last long, and at Repeal he began making and shipping bulk wines.

In 1934 he built the St. Helena plant for the production of dry wines and operated both plants until 1940, when he sold the Kingsburg plant and moved operations to Napa Valley, taking his savings of twelve years to begin quietly making and storing fine table wines. The wines released created a sensation overnight and put him among the ranks of California's top winemakers.

He acquired vineyards at St. Helena, southern Napa County and in Sonoma County. His most famous vineyard, called Monte Rosso from its red volcanic soil, is situated at 1000 feet elevation on the ridge dividing Napa and Sonoma Counties. This vineyard has produced some top quality wines, which bear the appellation "Mountain" on the label. In all, the family owns some 800 acres of prime varietal vineyards, the latest acquisition being in Chiles Valley.

He built a family home adjacent to the old stone winery where he cellared some of his first wines during the 30's.

A picture of this giant of the industry as he was in his prime is found in Dr. Angelo Pellegrini's "Americans by Choice." The senior Martini is depicted as dining robustly, drinking wines with gusto, enjoying fam-

Martini's Monte Rosso Vineyards.

ily, friends, home and work with an earthy yet urbane zest and love of life. He is shown working in the winery, exchanging with co-workers the flashes of temper that, among Italians, indicates "health, virility and love."

In appearance, Louis was a typical North Italian, fair haired and blue eyed, with broad shoulders and standing almost 6 feet tall. He prided himself on his cooking, as well as his wines, and as an octogenarian one of his favorite activities was preparing luncheon for his friends. His natural wine palate and nose, which he viewed as his greatest assets, were augmented by a lifetime—66 years—spent in their cultivation.

Although Louis M. Martini turned over the reins of the winery operation to his son Louis Peter in 1960, he maintained an office at the winery and came in every day until the last few months of his life. As is traditional in many European families, he was every inch the head of the family and business, the boss, as long as he lived.

The younger Martini is president of the firm which, in spite of its size—over two million gallons storage capacity—is still a personal one, reminiscent of the small, family-owned wineries in the valley. There is a strong family feeling among the employees, an aura of strength and continuity about the winery.

The red wines are robust and straightforward, with both character and potential. The Special Selection bottlings, available only at the winery and then in limited quantities, are very smooth and well-rounded, and carefully chosen for their potential to acquire the assets age can bring to a fine wine. Among the whites are a rare varietal Folle Blance, from the Monte Rosso vineyard, and an exceptional Gewurztraminer, a dry and spicy wine. A very delicate white wine is Moscato Amabile, sold only at the winery, slightly sweet and sometimes bubbly.

There are also generic wines, which those whose purse does not permit vintage wine on the table every day find very satisfying. The Mountain Red and Mountain White wines, from the Monte Rosso vineyard, are good everyday wines, forceful and pleasing. The line, all sold under the Louis M. Martini label, includes some 30 table and dessert wines.

The son, Louis P. Martini, has studied enology and viticulture at University of California's Berkeley and Davis campuses. He looks, in his middle years, a great deal like his famous father, with the same big frame, height and coloring. He has the same direct, straightforward way, believing sincerely in the dignity of hard work and that the making of fine wines is not done in a day. The Martinis believe that skillfull and judicious blending is the secret of making superior wines.

The Martinis live in the old Edge Hill winery, built in 1870, its two-foot-thick walls making a comfortable dwelling. There are two daughters and two sons, all interested in the winery. Louis P. plans and hopes that the family tradition of winemaking will be carried forward in their hands for the foreseeable future.

The fiery, dynamic head of the family is gone, but his influence on the wine community lingers, and he will not be forgotten when wine men foregather and old wine stories are recalled.

FRANCISCAN VINEYARDS

This redwood faced winery is located on Galleron Road, one mile north of Rutherford Crossroads. It is owned by a corporation formed in 1971 to set up a winery and vineyards.

President and chief executive officer is Harold W. Blakeley. Edmond Chaix is supervisor of the 250 acres of vineyards owned by Franciscan, and Leonard A. Berg is winemaker. Both are members of families identified with the wine industry over the years.

Chaix is a member of the family of French winemaker Jean Chaix. A. B. Brun and Chaix had a brisk sale for their Napa Valley wines in such sophisticated centers as New Orleans and New York at the turn of the century. The original Brun & Chaix stucco-front winery is on the east side of Highway 29 at Yountville; it was called Nouveau Medoc Cellars. Brun and Chaix were specialists in red wines, and had a reputation for scrupulous care in making their wines. The winery is now used by United Vintners for some of their Inglenook operations. The old Chaix home across the road is currently used as offices by Oakville Vineyards.

Berg is a nephew of Dr. Harold Berg, of the Department of Viticulture and Enology at University of California, Davis. Dr. Berg was honored for his contributions to the industry by the American Society of Enologists a few years ago.

The winery contains 22,000 square feet of space, which houses all facilities for fermenting, aging and bottling of the wines. There is a visitors' room at the front.

Cooperage for 300,000 gallons of wine storage includes large and small oak, and stainless steel. There is a projected capacity of 500,000 gallons estimated for 1975 and later.

Marketing is done through local shops and at the winery retail sales room. National distribution is planned for the near future.

The bottlings include Pinot Chardonnay, Sauvignon Blanc, Zinfandel, Carignane, Burgundy and a dessert wine, Muscato Canelli.

Vineyards from which these estate-bottled wines are made surround the winery, and there are two other Franciscan-owned vineyards, at Yountville, and in northeastern Napa near Redwood Road.

Berg feels that the future of Franciscan Vineyards and the valley in general is bright indeed. Large corporate wineries can exist side by side with small premium wineries, he says, and to the benefit of both. The small vintner with good local grapes can make his operation more efficient by keeping his cooperage filled with the more valuable wine, he believes, and adds that the U. S. market for premium wines has not yet been scratched.

This is one of the wineries which thinks favorably of some form of Appellation Controlee for Napa Valley. It can only benefit the industry, say the winery officials, and will guarantee the continued existence of the smaller vintner and grower interested in upgrading his product. This subject is being talked about extensively in the valley, but vintners are divided in their reaction.

LYNCREST VINEYARDS

Richard K. Lynn, a San Francisco management consultant, with seven partners, owns this small winery at the end of White Sulphur Springs Road. The dusty dirt road winds its way to the 60 acre mountain vineyard at 2000 feet elevation. It was bonded in 1972, and plans are to produce only a few varietal wines, Johannisberg Riesling, Chenin Blanc, Cabernet Sauvignon and Zinfandel. There is an 80-year old Zinfandel vineyard on the property, from which some interesting wine is expected, according to Winemaker John Henderson.

The firm bought the ranch, formerly belonging to J. W. Kramm, in 1968, and for the next years sold the grapes while assembling the winery and equipping it with a small amount of the best cooperage. It is deemed by wine men to be one of the finest and best equipped small wineries in the county. Fermenting is done on the first floor of the winery, which is a red barn-like building, and there is an air-conditioned cellar on the second floor. Projected capacity of the winery is 15,000 cases a year.

Lynn has always been interested in winery management, and has become a nationally recognized authority on the subject.

John Henderson, the winemaker, learned his craft from the master winemaker J. Leland Stewart during his years at Souverain Cellars on Howell Mountain. He worked with Stewart for several years, and has been with Lyncrest for the past two. His reputation is so well known that the owners find it appropriate to have his name on their label.

The winery building began life as a dairy barn, but has risen above its humble origins. Located on a small rise, there is room at the rear to build an 8,000 square foot cellar with two tunnels dug into the hillside for aging the wines. Work on this project will be under way in 1975.

There is a good market for super-premium wines, says Henderson, and it will increase, not diminish. There is a movement afoot to put some of the product of small wineries in wine shops across the country, and Lyncrest expects to avail itself of this opportunity for national distribution.

Wines are now on the market, selling at a moderately high price. There is no mailing list, but wines are distributed through some 30 retail outlets within the state.

Lynn got into the industry as an outgrowth of buying a summer home in the hills above Napa Valley. The property included a vineyard, and for years grapes were sold to Heitz Cellars, Robert Mondavi and Souverain Cellars. Eventually the winery came into being, and the Lynns spend every possible minute in the valley. They expect to divide their time between San Francisco and Napa Valley for the future.

The first Lyncrest wines have been well received at private tastings, including the Vintners Club, San Francisco. No reds will be released for some years yet.

This is a production winery, and there are no visitor facilities.

CHATEAU CHEVALIER

Beringer Brothers owned this gorgeous Spring Mountain vineyard until F. Chevalier purchased the property in 1884. The winery, described by Leon D. Adams as "one of the loveliest old stone cellars in the country" in his recent book, "The Wines of America," was built in 1891.

It was given to Chevalier's son George, with the elder Chevalier personally attending to all of the winery operations. He won acclaim for his wines, distributed throughout the nation, by 1889. The industry was well aware of his superior products, which included "Castle" brand wines, clarets and brandies. He maintained offices on North Main Street in Los Angeles, with headquarters on Washington Street in San Francisco.

The next major owners were Howard Hart and his family, long-time residents of the valley, who owned it from 1915 to 1940. Mr. and Mrs. Leslie Rogers maintained the estate for the next 22 years, lavishing love and care on the building and grounds. The wine market at that time did not warrant the restoration of the vineyards, but the formal gardens on the estate were brought back to a gracious splendor.

Rogers died in 1960, and Chateau Chevalier was purchased by a trio of investors, called "Chateau Chevalier Associates," in 1962. Their infrequent visits to the estate launched it into a period of neglect and disrepair; gardens returned to the wild state and the stone steps leading to the terraced vineyards became overgrown with weeds.

Happily the present owners, Gregory Bissonette, James Frew and Peter Hauschildt, purchased the Chateau in 1969, and brought new vigor and excitement to restoration of the handsome estate. Under their ownership, the 10,000 case winery made its first crush in 1973. The estate grown wine will be labeled Chateau Chevalier and will include Cabernet Sauvignon, Chardonnay, White Riesling and Pinot Noir. A secondary label, Mountainside Vineyards, will be a product reflecting the Chateaux ability to select and buy high quality grapes.

Their enthusiasm in reclaiming the abandoned vineyard and grounds was apparent on a recent visit to the famous Chateau. Gregory was driving the tractor down a row of terraced vines, with his young son, Gregory Jr., on his lap. Following the tractor was his wife Kathy and a Mexican helper. They were hurrying, just ahead of a winter rain, to abate future weed problems. It was an inspiring sight—a united young family working toward a worthy goal.

After tasting the wines at the Chateau, one can feel assured that the style and tradition of a family-owned and operated winery will continue to be reflected in the wines. The Bissonettes, who co-occupy the stone building along with the wines, are a large family—there are six children—and their intention is to make fine wine.

There is an aura about the place and the people that will please and inspire any visitor to the Chateau. A lapsed tradition has been revitalized, and will remain vigorous and growing for years to come.

YVERDON VINEYARDS

A long, narrow and stony road leads to this mountain winery in a wooded section on Spring Mountain near St. Helena. The owner, Fred J. Aves, with his son Russell, bought a 50-year old hillside vineyard in 1970, cleared the land which had grown up to firs and scrub oak, and planted 10 acres of new vines. They also have 80 acres of vines on Bennett Lane in Calistoga, called Rancho Alto.

The elevation is 2,000 feet. At the end of the road is the handsome cut stone winery, made by the hands of Fred and Russell Aves and helpers. They are making and marketing their first wines while building the winery and Fred's home, with their first crush in 1971.

Aves is a former Los Angeles business man, a manufacturer of auto supplies, and his son began his business career as a mechanic and builder of racing cars. From this incongruous background they turned to an interest in wine. Fred began making it in his home, with Southern California grapes, which he soon found did not meet his expectations. He began buying Napa Valley grapes and transporting them to Los Angeles to make his wine. This led to purchase of the Rancho Alto vineyard, which in turn led to selling out the Los Angeles holdings and moving the operation to Napa Valley.

The labor involved has been prodigious, cutting and laying each stone by hand. The winery is a castle-like structure in the old school of valley winery architecture, with Tudor arches, quatrefoil stained glass windows and similar features. The stone used is a hard grade engineer stone, from which many valley wineries were made in the 19th century. They are constructing hillside tunnels for aging the wines, an anacronistic procedure not followed by wineries built during the 20th century. Tunnel construction has been complicated by the necessity for shoring up the tunnel with concrete arches as they go.

Also under construction on the winery site is Fred's home, of cut stone, a two story structure with a mansard roof. Both the winery and the home were designed by Fred, without benefit of architect, along the lines of buildings he had admired in France.

The venture has been family-contained, with the exception of a laborer or two to help with rough work. Father and son have enjoyed and taken pride in creating something uniquely their own, with their own heads and hands. All hands fall to and work at the winery when the wines are ready—Fred, his son, Russell's wife Leona, and their two young sons and daughter. It is a life style all enjoy and accept with enthusiasm.

Fred is a man of parts; besides being able to design and create intricate buildings and make wine, he is also a super gourmet cook,—"Isn't everyone?" he asks, with no idea that the answer is, sadly, "No." He cooks as naturally as he makes wine, with no feeling that he is doing anything extraordinary. The only difficulty, he says, is geeting some of the needed ingredients for a favorite dish.

The winery has a capacity of 50,000 gallons, which they plan to bring to a 100,000 gallon level within a year or two.

BERINGER VINEYARDS

The Beringer story begins in the mid-1800's with Frederick and Jacob, members of a winemaking family from Mainz on the Rhine. The lure of French winemaking techniques brought them to the Medoc, and later, in 1870, Jacob met Frederick in New York to help in his established wine marketing business.

Although all went well with the brothers, they hungered for a vineyard and winery of their own. In a visit to St. Helena, some years later, Jacob found what he sought—just the location for winery and vineyard. Here was the ideal climate—warm, with sandy soil, soft sunshine, gentle rains, and at the end of the season, brisk winter weather that gave, he knew, exactly the right conditions for the growing of quality grapes.

He found the perfect spot to erect a winery, a hillside of soft stone, which formed the ideal environment for the aging of the fine wines he planned to produce.

In 1876 the brothers combined their talents and established the Beringer Brothers Winery. While the vineyards were being established and cellars constructed, Jacob was working at the Charles Krug Winery just down the road. Frederick built the Rhine House, a stately mansion which duplicated, as nearly as obtainable materials would allow, the old family castle on the Rhine. It remains today as a tourist attraction, as well as a tribute to Los Hermanos, The Brothers, whose desire was to produce fine wine.

The original winery was 40 by 104 feet, with walls of massive stone, and the ground floor slightly pitched to allow for drainage. Behind this three-story structure were tunnels carved into the volcanic stone hill. ·The Chinese provided the labor. Employing picks, shovels and sweat to remove segments of the stone, they carried out the rubble in small woven baskets, finally completing a thousand feet of tunnel.

The second story was built like the deck of a ship and caulked regularly. It was water tight, and could be flooded to a depth of several inches without a leak. The third floor was used for the crushing of grapes, employing the old technique of gravity flow during winery operations.

Horse-drawn wagons laden with grapes were led around a road at the rear of the winery to deliver their load to the crusher. The St. Helena Star reported in 1883: "The wine cellar of Beringer Bros. is large and substantial, and the most handsomely finished of any in the Napa Valley. For solidarity of build and completeness of appointments, it can have no superior anywhere. The monogram of the owners, B. B., is neatly cut in the keystone."

With the buildings completed and vineyards producing, the brothers set out to achieve their reputation for quality wine. Before Prohibition, awards were won in San Francisco in 1887; Paris in 1889 and 1900; Dublin in 1892 and Chicago in 1893.

The fame of Beringer Bros. wines and brandy continued for many years. In 1914 the survivors of the two brothers' families incorporated Beringer Bros. Several women of the family became officers of the corpora-

Oak barrels in Beringer's stone caves

tion. Bertha was president; Martha vice president; and Agnes Beringer Young, assistant secretary. Los Hermanos might properly have changed its name to Las Hermanas under their direction.

The name "Los Hermanos" was given the estate by a close friend, Senor Tiburcio Parrot, a Spanish gentleman of the old school, who lived in a beautiful villa above the Rhine House. They had a team of magnificent matched horses, as did the Beringers, and Miss Bertha Beringer, who wrote a history of the winery, recalls: "the elegant carriage, the sprinted team driven by a resplendent coachman in livery, in which Don Tiburcio and his lovely wife used to dash up the winding drive to call at the Rhine House."

Sr. Parrot's villa, called "Miravalle," is a replica, but on a larger scale, of the Beringer residence. The two families vied with one another in setting the pace for elegant appointments and gracious living.

For almost 100 years the winery was continously owned and operated by members of the Beringer family, and the title of "Napa Valley's oldest winegrowing family" can be accorded them. Since 1879 they produced every vintage, without exception, to Prohibition, for they supplied, and continue to supply, altar and medicinal wines for the clergy and medical professions throughout the country.

Young Fred Beringer, the fourth generation of the family, today owns and operates the Bottle Shop in St. Helena, and thus continues the family's traditional association with wine.

In 1970 the Beringer family sold the winery and 700 acres of vineyard to Nestle, Inc., the Swiss-based international food company. The present owner is listed as Crosse & Blackwell Vintage Cellars, a Nestle affiliate, guided by H. Robert Bras.

The Rhine House, once the center of gracious living for the Beringer family, has been fully restored to its rightful elegance. It serves as a hospitality center, so that all visitors to Beringer may view its splendors as a part of their wine tour.

Beringer is one of the most interesting valley wineries to visit because of the maze of stone tunnels cut a thousand feet into the hill behind the winery by picks of Chinese laborers. There are many beautiful wooden casks, hand carved with designs of a California grizzly, clusters of grapes and similar motifs.

Vineyards have been expanded to include 3,000 acres of vines either leased or owned in Napa, Knights and Alexander valleys. A new expansion of facilities is under way across the road (Highway 29). Since its acquisition by Nestle, no expense has been spared to upgrade the winery and holdings to a sound commercial basis.

The new winemaster at Beringer's is the highly regarded Myron Nightingale, who was a classmate at Berkeley of Louis P. Martini. He is said by William Massee to be "a legendary winemaker," having guided the destinies of Cresta Blanca and developed its famed Premier Semillon. Stephen O'Donnell and Larry Merla are his assistants. Nightingale is busy perfecting techniques that will insure that Beringer grapes produce traditional wines of highest quality, which they must now do in quanities large enough for national distribution.

CHRISTIAN BROTHERS WINERY

A world-reknown valley landmark is Greystone Cellars. It is approached through the "archway of the elms" just north of St. Helena, and is one of the homes of Christian Brothers wines. Two other facilities, one at Mont LaSalle, the other south of the town, are a part of the complex.

Christian Brothers is an order of the Roman Catholic Church, a group of laymen whose members live in community, take vows of poverty, chastity and obedience, and give their lives to serving others. The Brothers are dedicated to education of the young, with some thirteen secondary schools and colleges supported by Christian Brothers winemaking programs.

Greystone has an interesting history, and has played a major part in creating the valley wine empire. It was built in 1889 by William Bourn, a wealthy vineyard owner, who is still remembered in the valley for his generosity and community spirit. At the time it was built, Greystone was the largest stone winery in the world. The cost, fantastic for the time, was $2 million.

Bourn was owner of two Napa Valley vineyards, of San Francisco's Spring Valley Water Company, and had extensive mining interests. He conceived the idea of establishing a growers' cooperative, to make wine from the valley grapes, age it at Greystone, and lend growers the money, ten cents per gallon, to keep afloat until their wines could be matured and marketed. But un-

fortunately, this altruistic scheme came into being just as phylloxera got a foothold in the vineyards, and production of wine fell sharply.

Greystone had a procession of owners for the next fifty years. It was owned by Charles Carpy, Bisceglia Brothers, the California Wine Association, Central California Wineries, Cresta Blanca, and Roma Cellars. It was sold to Bisceglia during the Depression for an unbelievable $10,000—a building of three stories, measuring 400 by 78 feet, with a 20 by 50 foot projection at the front—a total floor space of just under three acres.

Exterior walls are hand-cut native sandstone, creating a structure of massiveness and beauty. There are Roman arches, high vaulted ceilings, huge doors and mahogany paneling. The aging facilities include imported white oak tanks of huge size, built on the site during construction of the winery. On the third floor, Champagne is produced by the Charmat method.

In 1945, the Christian Brothers, whose winery was at Martinez, leased cellar space from the owners, Roma Cellars, and in 1950 they purchased the winery outright, and moved their operation to the Napa Valley.

In the wooded hills above the valley is Mont LaSalle, an old stone winery built in 1903 by a German winemaker, Theodore Gier. The setting is one of exceptional beauty and charm, with vineyards marching up the hill, which is crowned by the handsome school and winery buildings. Here, between matins and vespers, wines are made, novices trained and visitors received. The gardens are spacious and picturesque, and the chanting in the chapel adds to a stroll among the flowers.

The winery's administrative offices are at the Mont

Mont la Salle Novitiate amidst 200 acres of vines.

La Salle location. In the lobby of the buildings are several handsome wood carvings of vineyard scenes. In one, a cowled and habited Brother is seen crushing grapes in a horse trough with a wooden club.

There is another new facility just south of St. Helena, a tribute to the far-sighted policies and shrewd business acumen of the Order. Forseeing the wine explosion in its infancy, the new complex was begun in 1965 with a warehouse which became inadequate for their expanded needs by the time it was completed. The Brothers determined to "think bigger," and made this structure the first unit of a five-phase building program. The plan is a daisy pattern, with buildings raying out from a circular center. Further segments of the expansion include buildings to house laboratories, tasting and sales rooms, warehouse space, bottling facilities, administrative offices and a large area for holding special events. Everything is designed to make, age and ship wine as efficiently as possible, with all winemaking processes fully automated.

Cellarmaster is Brother Timothy, one of the industry's most colorful figures. He has been with the Order for 46 years, involved with wines since 1935. He knows the wine business thoroughly, from planting the vine to writing the label, and has done both.

Brother Tim's internationally famous collection of corkscrews has a representative display at Greystone, along with early day presses and other winemaking equipment. He is perhaps one of the most interviewed and photographed men in the wine world, and is never too busy to talk about the Order or the wines.

His winemaking theories differ from some other valley wineries, in that his talents are directed to making the end product as uniform as possible, from year to year. The genial Brother Tim has a famous palate, and wines are blended, from two or three vintages, to produce as perfect a wine, with identifiable varietal characteristics, as can be done. Blending is always done with an eye to quality, and the result is that a bottle of any Christian Brothers wine will be the same dependable quality, year in and year out. All wines are moderately priced.

The Christian Brothers operation is the largest in Napa Valley, in point of physical size as well as production-wise, with a capacity of three and one-half million gallons of table and sacramental wines. Over 200,000 visitors pass the famous Greystone portals every year. Visitor facilities are maintained at both Greystone and Mont LaSalle, and tours and visits are eminently worthwhile.

Christian Brothers wines, Champagnes and brandies are marketed through the firm of Fromm & Sichel. The Wine Museum in San Francisco is a joint effort of the Brothers and their marketing firm, and is a mecca for visitors from the world wine scene. Gathered together there are many treasures depicting various phases of wine and wine art, handsomely housed and beautifully displayed. The Museum is a must on the agenda of all wine country visitors.

The wines produced by Christian Brothers comprise a full line of varietal and generic types, as well as Vermouth, brandy and Champagne. Their vineyards cover about 1000 acres in Napa Valley, and another 1000 acres in the San Joaquin Valley.

SPRING MOUNTAIN VINEYARDS

This winery was founded in 1968, using as its headquarters the basement of a century-old home just north of Christian Brothers at St. Helena. The stately Victorian mansion was built in 1876 by Fritz Rosenbaum, a San Francisco glass merchant, and called Johannaberg Vineyards.

Vineyards and buildings had fallen into disrepair, but caught the eye and imagination of Michael Robbins, an engineer from Iowa with a law background, during a busines trip to the valley in 1963. He spent the next years restoring it, and assembled a winemaker's dream of a winery in its below-level basement. His first Spring Mountain wine was introduced in 1970.

By 1974, ready for expansion of his facilities, Mike bought the Tiburcio Parrot home and winery, Miravalle, located on a hillside off Spring Mountain Road. The elegant old estate crowns a little rise, and as the name implies, commands a view of the valley.

A member of a banking and finance family, Parrot believed in the valley as superlative wine country, and in hillside vineyards as growing the finest grapes. He planted his vineyards, the choicest French varieties, as high as horse and plow could go. He produced a very fine Margaux, which won honors among knowledgeable wine lovers of the day.

This handsome property was purchased from the Parrot estate by Wallace Hyde, who owned it until its sale to Robbins. The house is a larger facsimile of the Rhine House or Beringers, of whom Parrot was a friend and contemporary.

The redwood winery building, with its 90 feet of caves dug into the hillside, will be torn down and a new winery built, of an architectural style akin to other valley wineries.

The first Spring Mountain wines, a Chardonnay and a Sauvignon Blanc released in 1970, were proclaimed excellent by connoisseurs. He has also released a Cabernet Sauvignon with great promise. The 1973 crush yielded 6,500 cases, and the winery output will continue to increase to reach an estimated capacity of 15,000 cases when the vines are mature. Replanting of the Miravalle vineyards will begin at once, says Mike.

Mike Robbins' devotion to detail has won him fame in his dual professions of engineering and law. He is presently commuting between Los Angeles and Napa Valley, and this will continue until winery production warrants giving it his full attention. His winemaker is Charles Ortman. The family, including two young sons, are winery workers.

Both Mike and Shirley feel the valley is a great place to make fine wine because of climate and soil, and "a great tradition which motivates winemakers to achieve the highest form of the winemaker's art." The future, they believe, is very bright.

The proliferation of small wineries is an ecological as well as an economic asset, they say. It is, in the widest meaning of the words, the highest and best use of this national asset.

CHARLES KRUG WINERY

This winery, said to be the oldest in Napa Valley, was established by Charles Krug in 1861. He was a pioneer wine man whose influence reached far beyond the valley. He was the first Viticultural Commissioner for the district of Napa, and was known for his prodigality of sympathy, kindliness and geniality. In his day the winery was known as "Chateau Krug," with its majestic oaks, old-time rambling buildings and air of homely comfort.

Charles Krug was born in Prussia, emigrated to the USA at age 22, and then returned to his native land briefly to participate in an attempt to overthrow a reactionary government. The revolt failed, Krug was imprisoned, but made a dramatic escape and fled to Philadelphia, pursued by state police.

Krug came to San Francisco in 1852 and worked on a newspaper there until he met Agoston Haraszthy, who influenced him to get into viticulture. He bought 20 acres in Sonoma County and planted vines. That same year, using a small cider press, he made 1200 gallons of wine in Napa Valley. This established him as a proficient winemaker, and his services were in demand.

In 1860 he moved to St. Helena and settled on the present winery site, where he planted a vineyard and built his first wine callar. One stone wall of this original winery is still standing.

Krug was a California wine enthusiast, devoted whole-heartedly to upgrading the industry. Never daunted by phylloxera, depression or past blunders, he gave his life and an ample fortune to developing the industry and improving the wines. Fortunately he lived to see Napa Valley lead the state in production of fine wines. With his dedication to all that was progressive, he left a legacy of high standards in conduct and achievements to the industry.

After his death the ranch was run by his two daughters, Lolita and Linda, and later by a nephew, who made wine up to the time of Prohibition. After Repeal, the vineyards and cellars were leased to Napa Wine Co. until they were sold to the Cesare Mondavi family in 1943.

The operation has been in the hands of the Mondavis ever since that time. Cesare was an Italian immigrant who came to America and worked in the iron mines in Minnesota. He returned to Italy to marry his childhood sweetheart and bring her back to the U.S.A. Their four children, Mary, Helen, Robert and Peter, were born in the mid-west.

In 1922 Cesare came to California, settling at Lodi and going into the wholesale fruit business, a successful venture. When Repeal came he was ready to begin winemaking, and looked about for a location in Napa Valley, where he shrewdly deemed the future of fine wines lay. Both his sons had studied enology, and he was thinking of their future. The Sunny St. Helena Winery, at the south edge of town, was first acquired and added to his operations at Lodi and Fresno. Later he purchased the Krug estate, and the family faced together the challenge of rehabilitation and expanding the winery. It was at

6000 oak barrels stacked for aging.

this juncture that the Mondavis realized their ambition of converting their operation from a bulk winery to one of bottled premium varietal wines. Old vineyards were pulled out, and vines replaced with better quality varieties. His wines began to receive recognition.

At his death in 1959, his heirs owned one of the finest and best equipped wineries in the country. Rosa Mondavi took her husband's place as head of the family and president of C. Mondavi & Sons. She and her children are directors and sole owners of the capital stock of the corporation. Peter, a graduate of Stanford University with post-graduate courses in viticulture and enology, became general manager and vice president of the company. He is currently its winemaker, assisted by George Vierra.

Peter Mondavi believes in family winery ownership as the best way to achieve fine wines of consistent high quality. The winery, although large (3,500,000 storage capacity) has kept the individual touch, and a glow of pride in achievement that is immediately felt at the winery.

In the 30-odd years of Mondavi ownership there have been some changes. The size, scope and efficiency of the cellars have been greatly augmented, with the most up-to-date equipment and modern technology introduced. Additional acreage has been acquired and planted to the finest varietals, with 1200 acres in Napa Valley planted to Cabernet Sauvignon, Pinot Noir, Gamay Beaujolais, Pinot Chardonnay, Johannisberg Riesling and Gewurztraminer.

In 1966, Robert Mondavi left the firm to establish his own winery further down the valley. Peter remains to hold Mondavi aims, policies and goals to the high standard set by his father, and before him, by Charles Krug.

"To make fine wine, there must be modern equipment and technology," says Peter Mondavi, "and also the human element must be maintained. The old-timers believed and quality of the man's wine depended on his own quality and character. A little bit of himself goes into every bottle. To gain lasting fame, a winemaker must be a poet, a philosopher, an honorable man, as well as a master craftsman."

Two labels are used at Charles Krug Winery, the Charles Krug brand of varietal and generic wines bottled in fifths and tenths, and the CK brand, varietal and generic wines available in these sizes and also in gallons and half-gallons. Wines are distributed nationally.

The advance of dry winemaking technology in this area, says Peter, has attracted and continues to attract the best winemakers. If those establishing wineries in the valley do the right job, planting the right grapes in the right area, with a winemaker who can put it all together, their wines will always find a market. However, he points out, people entering the industry should realize that establishing a label takes many years, years filled with hard work and frustration.

It is rumored that the family has turned down some tempting offers to sell out. They continue to resist, for the feeling for the traditions of an old family winery is strong in the Mondavi clan.

The winery buildings are of turn-of-the century vintage, and music festivals and many other community events are held each year on its wide, oak-fringed lawns.

BURGESS CELLARS

This stone and redwood winery was built about 1875. It is located on Howell Mountain east of St. Helena, at about 1100 feet elevation, and was part of the original Rossini homestead. It was purchased in 1943 as a retirement avocation, by J. Leland Stewart, who founded Souverain Cellars.

Stewart restored the old 30-acre Rossini vineyards, remodeled and enlarged the winery, and commissioned the handsome carved wooden doors, the work of artist Merrill Abbott. The work depicts a vintage scene. During the Stewart regime, additional structures were added including a bottle binning storage room.

Stewart set himself to learn winemaking, aided by UC Davis enologists and neighboring vintners, including Andre Tchelistcheff, and during the next years laid down some superlative vintages. He produced the first varietal Green Hungarian wine, a winner of Gold Medals at fairs and expositions.

Winemaking is a man-killing job, Stewart decided, leaving little leisure to enjoy the fruits of his labors. He sold the winery in 1970, after 25 successful vintages, to a group of investors, who resold the facility in 1972. Current owner is Thomas E. Burgess of New York and Ohio, a former corporation airplane pilot. He rechristened the winery "Burgess Cellars," and plans to carry on in the Stewart tradition. He has added a laboratory and office to the facility and his first wines are on the market now, the work of winemaker Bill Sorensen. Bill, a native of Missouri, graduated from Fresno in 1972 where he was in charge of the experimental winery. Their eight varietals have received the personal attention only available at a family owned and operated winery.

Burgess Cellars wines are made from plantings on his own acres, plus grapes bought from selected vineyards in the area. The new owner is dedicated to making good wines and to bringing out the special character of each wine his hillside vineyards can produce. The winery is small, 12,000 cases annually, and young, with the future still to be determined. It will depend, in part, on his ability to find and purchase enough grapes from local growers of quality varietals to fill out the capabilities of his winery.

Burgess vineyards are planted to Cabernet Sauvignon, Zinfandel, Petite Sirah, Grenache and Berger and include approxamately 22 acres.

"We have to find growers who are as interested as we are in knowing that beautiful wine is made from their grapes," comments Burgess. He is confident that whatever effort this entails, Burgess Cellars is willing and able to make. The intent to produce superior varietal wines, and to continue living the life of a family involved with winemaking, is of utmost importance to Tom and Linda Burgess.

Wines are sold only at the winery and a few selected retail shops. Patrons are invited to drop in at the winery and share a picnic area overlooking a panoramic view of the entire Northern Napa Valley and surrounding mountains.

POPE VALLEY WINERY

This rustic building on Pope Valley Road is one of the **few** gravity flow wineries left **in** California. It is three stories high, built into the hillside **behind,** taking advantage of **the** terrain for temperature control.

The winery was founded by Sam Haus in 1909, and operated with his sister Lily under the name "Sam Haus Winery" until his retirement in 1959. Sam achieved a certain local distinction for his undying war on rattlesnakes; now retired, he still pursues them relentlessly on trips to the country.

After his retirement, the winery was idle until 1972, when it was bought by its present owners, James and Arlene Devitt.

The winery represents a bit of old California history. Its timbers are of redwood, salvaged from the old Oat Hill Mine, a Napa County quicksilver mine of the 1880's. This mine was located near the Mountain Mill House, now a Girl Scout camp, which was then a stagecoach relay stop and inn for travelers to Lake County. The setting is picturesque, among valley oaks, built partly over a live stream. The Devitts have completely renovated the building, replacing all equipment and cooperage with new, modern fittings, yet still retaining the natural charm.

In its early days the building was designed to receive grapes on the top (third) floor. They were then conveyed to the second floor, where the crusher and fermenters were located. After its fermentation period, the wine was racked, by gravity, into storage tanks in the cellar on the first floor. Here the wine was aged before being racked once more into smaller 50-gallon barrels for shipment to eastern markets for bottling and distribution.

Today the procedure is the same, except that wines are aged in small cooperage, and bottled at the winery. Some wines have been released in Northern and Southern California as well as at the winery and the Pope Valley General Store. Capacity of the winery is 60,000 gallons storage. Wines include generic and varietal types.

The winery has another claim to fame, which makes it relatively easy to locate—it is across the road from another valley landmark, the Litto Damonte place. This folk artist has fashioned a setting from thousands of old hub caps, spiced with old tires, washing machines, plumbing fixtures, bird houses, windmills and wishing wells. Once seen it can never be forgotton, and the creator of this masterpiece enjoys having visitors stop in to chat and exclaim.

Devitt, a former hobby winemaker, is still involved with his electronics business, but expects to become a full time winemaker in due course. The winery is open on weekends, and is a pleasant place to visit, with picnic tables, hiking area and renovated blacksmith shop. The Devitts are proud to point out the ranch was entirely self sufficient in the past and the old steam boiler which once powered the ranch can still be seen. Interested wine buffs may drop in to talk with the proprietor, taste and buy available vintages. An aura of timelessness prevails, reminiscent of an earlier, simpler day.

FREEMARK ABBEY WINERY

1971
NAPA VALLEY

JOHANNISBERG
RIESLING

Produced and Bottled by
FREEMARK ABBEY WINERY, ST. HELENA, CALIFORNIA
Alcohol 13.6% by volume

Freemark Abbey Winery was built in 1895 by Antonio Forni, a newly-arrived Italian, who used blocks of stone cut by hand from the surrounding area. He opened the winery, called Lombarda Cellars, and continued operation until 1922, when it was sold to Patrick Murphy and James J. Mahoney. In 1938 it reverted to the widow of the founder, who sold it to Albert M. Ahern. Ahern first called it "Freemark Abbey." He made, in addition to wines, wine vinegar and wine jellies which enjoyed local fame.

In 1965 the property, then owned by Ben Swig of hotel fame and no longer operating as a winery, was sold again, this time coming to the present owners, a limited partnership involving seven men. They reactivated the winery in 1967. Charles Carpy, one of the owners, is the grandson of an earlier Charles Carpy who operated the Uncle Sam Wine Cellars at Napa in the 1880's. This winery made a large quantity of wine, champagne and brandy, with national distribution of the products.

Other local grower-owners are Frank Wood, William Jaeger, James Warren, the prestigious wine consultant Brad Webb, and Richard Heggie and John Bryan of the Bay Area. The winemaker is Jerry Luper, a graduate of Fresno State School of Enology, who formerly worked for E. & J. Gallo at Modesto, later for a valley winery, Louis M. Martini.

The new owners planted choice varietals in two vineyards in the Rutherford area, Red Barn Ranch and the Carpy-Wood vineyards. From the start they were interested in producing fine wine by as natural methods as possible. Their winemaking operation is based on the concept that, under proper conditions, wine makes itself. Through controlled environment the wine is put through processes of crushing, pressing and fermentation, using a stainless steel, garolla-type stemmer-crusher, a rotating bladder press, and fermentation tanks encased in cooling jackets.

They prefer to minimize such interferences as filtration, heavy fining and complex stabilization procedures in an effort to retain all the flavor inherent in the grapes. All their Cabernets are blended with Merlot. Their red wines are aged in small oak cooperage from 12 to 18 months, released four years from vintage. Whites are released two years after vintage, with six months of bottle age.

Their wines, produced from grapes grown by the owners themselves, by the most approved methods of viniculture, have received favorable notice from wine enthusiasts, and have been compared favorably with the best French vintages. Harry Waugh, the British connoisseur, calls their 1968 Cabernet Bosche (from a special vineyard) "a splendid achievement."

The mossy stone cellar has a restaurant, gourmet shop and candle factory on the upper floor. Recently added to the facility is a large building at the rear, housing bottle storage, bottling room, laboratory, visitor accommodations and retail sales room.

Freemark Abbey is a small winery, production for any given year planned not to exceed 50,000 gallons.

STONY HILL VINEYARDS

Fred and Eleanor McCrea established this small but exceedingly prestigious operation in 1951, and have since marketed wine to a small clientele reached via their own mailing list. Rare wineshops may occasionally have a few bottles, but they are few and far between. Each year's wines, two or three superb whites, are announced in early fall, released about November, and sold immediately. There is never enough to fill the great demand. These wines are said to be the best of their types grown in the area. Interested buyers are prompted to order them well in advance to insure delivery.

The winery and home are situated at the crest of an oak clad hill, seven hundred feet up in the Mayacamas Range, between Diamond Mountain on the north and Spring Mountain on the south, reached only by a winding road. The winemaker at Stoney Hill is Michael Chelini. There are no tasting facilities open to the public, but those with a previous appointment may visit the winery.

Stony Hill and its production have remained small over the years by the owners' choice. This is one of the most inspiring operations in California winemaking history, and the vineyard and winery have prompted many others to try the same kind of preferred life style and business combined. The 29 acres of vines are planted on hillsides, with their roots in thin, rocky soil, and there is no irrigation or frost control. The vineyard is in a warm belt, protected by the contour of the land.

McCrea is one of the pioneer escapees from big business, coming to the valley in 1943 to establish a summer home. He was an advertising agency executive who knew nothing of winemaking. He determined to use the extra space to grow something, and on the advice of his neighbors, settled on grapes. He sought help from the University of California, who advised him to plant Chardonnay. His 30 acres are planted to Chardonnay, White Riesling, Traminer and Semillon.

Although McCrea is not a pioneer in Napa Valley in the usual sense of the word, he is perhaps now, with the death of Louis Martini, the dean of family winemakers in the valley, as most the older family-owned wineries have gone the corporate route since 1964.

Over the years the McCreas planted, grew grapes, and made their first wines in the family kitchen, experimenting until the results satisfied them that they were ready to open the winery, a small building over the hill from the vineyards. Fred gives a high rating to established Napa Valley vintners who came to his assistance in those first years of winemaking, which resulted in some outstanding vintages laid down over the years. The advice to plant Chardonnay proved sound, and he had the satisfaction of seeing his two-year-old Chardonnay receive a Gold Medal at the California State Fair.

Aging of the Stony Hill white wines is done in small French and German oak cooperage, with a total capacity of about 7,000 gallons.

Stony Hill is a tiny winery, one of the smallest in Napa Valley, but it has had a great influence on the industry here and has acquired a well-deserved fame.

KORNELL CHAMPAGNE CELLARS

This winery, built in the 1880's by the Salmina family who operated it as the Larkmead Winery for many distinguished years, has had several owners since, and it later became Larkmead Cooperative Winery.

Hanns Kornell, fourth generation of a champagne-making family, brought his champagne operation to the valley after eight years in Sonoma County. He married a Napa Valley girl, Marilouise Rossini, and the couple, with their young son and daughter, form another of the valley's totally involved winery families. Paula serves as a wine tour guide, and young Peter Hanns, not yet in his teens, opens wine, sits in on tastings and selections, and hands visitors his own business card with aplomb.

Hanns came from Germany, where he worked in the champagne vineyards and cellars of both his father and grandfather. He left in 1939, arriving in this country, as he likes to say, "with $2 and an old suitcase." He studied at Geisenheim Enological Institute, and later worked at winemaking in France, Italy and England. He hitchhiked from New York to California, where he worked first as a laborer, later at Fountaingrove winery in Sonoma County. From this humble start he has made himself one of the state's most respected champagne makers, with more than one and one half million bottles in various stages of development. In 1952 he leased an old winery, made champagne by night and sold it by day, until he had enough money to buy Larkmead, now Kornell Cellars.

The winery is a square cement building, with the same forthright stability as its owner. Hanns believes in good grapes as the foundation of all he is trying to do, and chooses with religious devotion the still wines from which he makes his cuvees—Riesling, Chardonnay, White Pinot and Semillon. He has no vineyards, buys grapes and wines, and from them makes champagne in the traditional "in this bottle" method. His Sehr Trocken is the most dry, made by extra long aging from a specially developed cuvee, and has won plaudits since its appearance in 1972. Blending, a good palate, and training from early youth by grandfather, father and uncles is the secret of the Kornell champagne success.

There is also Kornell himself, who brings to champagne making all the vigor and elan of the bubbly itself. He enjoys what he is doing, asks no more of life than that it permit him to go on making and enjoying champagnes with his family. He has a tremendous faith in the future of the valley as a great and enduring wine country. He finds no generation gap with youth, his own or those hired for the winery; he is a brisk, efficient employer who expects, and gets, the best from his employees.

He is a winemaker in the old tradition, the tradition of Jacob Schram and Gustave Niebaum. He prefers to work for himself, with all this implies for a small business today, and to be independent, his own man in his own setting. He has cheerfully refused many offers, some of fantastic proportions, to sell his winery, and hopes to have his children continue after him.

SCHRAMSBERG VINEYARDS

Jacob Schram came to America in 1842, and reached Napa Valley in 1862. He worked as an itinerant barber, but had his mind on wine. Soon the barber had saved enough money to acquire a mountainside of his own. His wife Annie and the hard working Chinese planted the vines while Jacob went from farm to farm, plying his scissors.

Hard work paid off. He built the sturdy Victorian house, capacious stables, and extensive caves. Robert Louis Stevenson visited him in 1880 and said he looked "the picture of prosperity." The engaging tale is told in "The Silverado Squatters." His wines gained acclaim, and were served at famous hotels and clubs in California and abroad.

Schram died in March 1905 and was succeeded by his son Herman, who operated the winery until Prohibition, when it was sold for a summer home. After Repeal and two abortive ownerships, it was purchased by the Jack Davies organization in 1965.

A young career man on his way up, Jack Davies met the San Francisco Wine and Food Society and his gourmet wife Jamie in the 1950's. These events marked the beginning of his lifelong affinity for elegant wines.

Friends took the couple to visit Martin Ray in Saratoga, an unforgettable experience. Their host appeared to welcome them, "looking like Bacchus and acting like Bacchus," Davies recalls. They sat down to luncheon, which merged into dinner with no visible line of demarcation. Champagne flowed freely. "The occasion burned itself into my memory," says Davies, who later became an investor in Ray's Mt. Eden Vineyards.

Seeking a similar way of life for himself, he decided to leave Los Angeles and the big business scene for a vineyard of his own. A visit to Napa Valley and to Schramsberg ended his search for the right place. It was plentifully supplied with caves; champagne seemed the answer. Help came from such knowledgeable wine men as Fred McCrea, Andre and Dmitri Tchelistcheff and Dr. Maynard Amerine. He was impressed with the Stony Hill operation; the quality of the wines, the uncompromising excellence this small enterprise had achieved. He saw a great opportunity to make an American champagne with the prestige of the French.

By shrewd management and hard work, Davies has made champagne that occupies a place of honor in the world of fine wine. He and Jamie have restored the fine old house; he has been busy with endless details of vinyard and cellars, purchasing, shipping, planning. He finds the life as satisfying as he had envisioned it to be. Wine, he believes, brings back to life something that has been slipping away, and he is determined not to lose that something, for himself and for his family.

To succeed as a small winery, he says, one must know what he wants to do and how he is going to do it, and not try to have a foot in both camps. His goal: As wide distribution as possible of a smallish amount of superlative champagne. "If we get big enough to cut per-unit cost appreciably," he says, "we will have lost our reason for being—uniqueness."

123

STONE GATE WINERY

Stonegate is located on Dunaweal Lane just off Highway 29 at Calistoga, in the shadow of its larger hilltop neighbor, Sterling Winery. It was founded in the spring of 1973 by two families long interested in grapes and winemaking — Paul and June Landeros, James and Barbara Spaulding.

Paul Landeros is a long-time grower in Napa Valley, with some 30 years of involvement with vineyards, and vineyard development and management. He has planted vineyards for some of the premium wineries of the valley, and served as consultant on vineyard planning. He presently manages more than 500 acres of prime vineyards.

The Spauldings, by contrast, are newcomers to the valley. They came five years ago from Wisconsin, where Spaulding was for some 20 years medical science writer for the Milwaukee Journal. He has experimented extensively with both European vines and French hybrids. He bought vineyard land in the hills west of Calistoga in 1969, while he was at UC Berkeley, teaching journalism. Landeros was called upon to develop the Spaulding vineyards, and the possibility of a winery took shape.

Stonegate plans to produce its wines chiefly from grapes grown on steep hillside vineyards, such as those owned by Spaulding, where the crop is small but of superior quality. The first wine produced at Stonegate, a 1973 Chenin Blanc, was made chiefly from grapes grown in the Landeros-managed vineyards.

The winery is small and currently under construction. It is a long building with few architectural pretentions, for the two principals, together with General Manager John Swetland and Spaulding's son David, are busily concentrating on equipping the winery and making the wine. Equipment has been carefully chosen to apply the latest knowledge on fermentation and aging, but the founders intended to respect the centuries-old traditions of European winemaking, handling grapes with care, tending the wine meticulously, using a minimum of processing.

They were pleased with their first bottling, a 1973 dry Chenin Blanc, with much of the Loire grapes' pungent fruity character. It is a wine that will improve with a few year's bottle age, says Spaulding.

Stonegate's consulting winemaker is Robert Stemmler of Healdsburg, an enologist who studied at Bad Kreuznach, Germany, and worked in German vineyard operations and wineries for five years before he came to California 13 years ago. He has since guided wine production in some of Napa Valley's most prestigious premium wineries.

Winemaking procedures at Stonegate call for aging white wines in French oak cooperage, and European oak tanks. The red wines are aged in oak barrels, mostly French. Most of the wines of Stonegate will be estate bottled, some from hillside vineyards, some from the valley floor. It is a small, premium winery, carefully engineered for wine quality improvement and ease in operation.

STERLING VINEYARDS

Sterling Winery, near Calistoga, was founded in 1969 by Sterling International, a paper company with factories in many parts of the world. It is owned by three families, Peter L. Newton, Michael P. W. Stone and Ned Skinner.

The project had its beginnings in 1964, when the men of Sterling decided it was time they owned some land in the United States. They looked about, discovered Napa Valley, and established summer homes.

After some exposure to the wine industry, they were intrigued by it. They visited the University at Davis, viewed operations in South Africa and Australia. They decided that, by applying sound business principles, they could succeed in the wine industry. Land was acquired and planted to fine varietal grapes; vineyards consist of 400 acres in the upper valley, within three miles of the winery.

By 1968 they had enough vineyards to insure a supply of quality grapes, and began to study ideas for the winery. They had in mind something suited to the site, with esthetic appeal, not a hobby winery but a profitable business operation. A 100,000 case winery seemed about right.

The building that evolved is unique. The site is one of great natural beauty, a wood-fringed knoll between Silverado Trail and Highway 29. The building is the concept of Martin Waterfield, who wanted to recall the architecture of the Mediterranean. It is a simple, white structure, entirely functional, taking advantage of site possibilities to give California's most picturesque wine valley a creation of dignity and charm. There is a hint of the monastic, with stained glass windows, arches, carved doors and bells. The first plan was to top the building with a dove-cote, but this idea was discarded for bell towers in the interests of sanitation. The bells were cast in 1740, and once pealed from St. Dunstan's-in-the-East, London. Thme winery is reached by tram-cars from the valley. The yellow gondolas, transporting four visitors at a time, are now a familiar valley sight.

Sterling is one of the few Napa Valley wineries to be completely visitor-oriented from its inception. The interior is functional, with hospitality in mind. Visitors making the no-guide tour may view operations in the winery from a walkway above. A large upper deck commands a sweeping view of vine-clad valley and hills, and community functions are held there. There is something to delight all of the senses—the trees, fountains, bells, sculpture and flowers, plus the pungent smell of wine sleeping in tanks and barrels. The tasting room, farthest up the slope, has a roofed deck for enjoying the dramatic view.

The array of winemaking equipment is impressive. The latest and best of equipment and technology are employed by enologist R. W. Forman who, produced his first vintage in 1969, one year after receiving his masters degree at U.C. Davis. From its inception, the winery promised to produce some outstanding and innovative wines, and Forman, has justified the hopes placed in him by the Sterling owners.

CUVAISON CELLARS

This imposing new winery is a monument to the tenacity, foresight and hard work of a dedicated young man, Dr. Thomas Cottrell. Tom is a former laser physicist from Santa Clara County, who, with an engineer friend and fellow winelover, Thomas Parkhill, came to the valley in April, 1970. The name devised for the winery, "Cuvaison," is a French word meaning the fermenting of red wines on the skins of grapes.

They acquired a vineyard and had winemaking equipment installed in time for the crush, working, stripped to the waist in the hot July sun, to get foundations in, concrete poured and ready for crusher and tanks. With the deadline of harvest only days away, they toiled with fervor during 16-hour days.

Facilities that first year consisted of a concrete pad with equipment and a remodelled farmhouse used as office and tasting room. Parkhill later left the winery operation, and Cottrell went on alone, bottling and marketing his first vintage made from the short crop of 1970, which suffered major frost damage.

In 1973, a main arm of the Thorne family represented by C. T. Corporation, with a firm belief in the future of the valley, convinced Cottrell that they should become involved with his winery. This produced something he needed—ready capital, always in short supply at a budding winery. Construction of the spacious new winery on Silverado Trail followed. It has been provided with fully automated equipment of the finest design and manufacture, with sufficient space and facilities to expand operations from 10,000 gallons to 50,000 gallons capacity.

The building, which tops a little rise on the east side of the valley, is of California Mission style architecture, white stucco with red tile roof. The stained glass windows of modern design duplicate the winery label in color and style. At the front of the winery, near the highway, is a small tasting room and visitors' facility, site of the original farm house, where the public is welcomed and wines may be sampled.

Vineyards owned by Cuvaison are some 30 acres near Calistoga, planted to Napa Gamay, Cabernet Sauvignon, and Pinot Noir. Grapes for other wines are purchased locally to make their varietal dry wines.

Cuvasion has established a reputation, in the short time they have been in the valley, for interesting and innovative wines. They were one of the first to produce a Nouveau, a red wine made from their first crush, designed to be drunk young, in keeping with the custom in European vineyards to make a wine to enjoy at the harvest. The first Nouveau was fresh, fruity and slightly spritzy, made from Gamay grapes.

Creating and establishing a new label in the midst of the prestigious long-established appellations in which the valley abounds is acknowledged to be an enviable achievement for any young winemaker. Among his colleagues in the valley Tom Cottrell has made himself liked and respected in the few years he has been here.

DIAMOND CREEK VINEYARDS

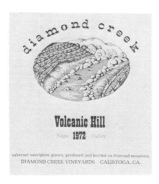

Albert Brounstein, a former owner of Standard Drug Distributors in Los Angeles and marketing man for Sebastiani and Weibel, bought and cleared the land on Diamond Creek six years ago. He has planted the 20 acres entirely to Cabernet Sauvignon and a small amount of Merlot for blending.

Al found, by soil analysis, three distinct soil types on the property, and the grapes from each will be made into three different estate-bottled Cabernet Sauvignons. The three are called Red Rock Terrace, Volcanic Hill and Gravelly Meadow vineyards, respectively, and each "vineyard within a vineyard" will have its own special label, showing the soil of origin.

Fermenting is done in redwood, aging in Nevers oak, and the wines are neither fined nor filtered.

By 1976 there will be some 6000 gallons ready to release. The first vintage, 1972, is being released in 1974, and is already committed to purchasers, except for a small amount retained for the Brounsteins and their friends.

Al and Boots Brounstein believe in the valley with fervor, especially their own corner of it, as the place to produce Cabernet Sauvignon, that most exquisite product of the noble vines. Youth, dedication and zeal are involved in their venture.

Their theories of marketing are their own, and include inviting groups of wine-oriented people to picnic on a woodland lake, created by damming Diamond Creek. The lake, with its grassy tree-shaded banks, is picturesque and invites swimming and boating as an adjunct to partaking of good food and wine. After exposure to the charms of the zestful Brounsteins and their outdoor guest facilities, visitors may place their names on a mailing list, to be informed when wines are ready to be released. Al estimates the increase in customers needed each year to sell all the wine produced numbers in the hundreds and based entirely upon Diamond Creek's bearing acreage. The output will never be large, and will be limited exclusively to their Cabernet Sauvignon.

At present the Brounsteins are renting an old stone winery from a neighboring rancher. The building was constructed by Chinese laborers, and its facade bears the date "1888." After years of disuse, the Brounsteins cleared the building for their own wines, and are now aging two vintages in its root-tangled stone caves cut 100 feet back into the hills. It is naturally cool, the two-foot thick stone walls never allowing the temperature to rise above 60 degrees, nor fall below 55.

However, they are eager to get to work on their own winery, and are scheduled to begin its construction in 1975.

The new winery building, of stone and redwood, will, when complete, be tucked into a niche between two earthen hillocks and will provide them with quarters on its upper floor. Al likes to think of it as being designed along the same functional lines as Hanzell Winery. The site overlooks the vineyards, and is ringed about by woods of pine, fir, madrone and considerable stand of fine second-growth redwoods.

CHATEAU MONTELENA

Chateau Montelena, at the foot of Mount St. Helena in Calistoga, has a spectacular setting. It is an old winery, the label dating back to 1882. It was constructed by Alfred A. Tubbs, a New Englander who came from New York to California in 1850, and founded the Tubbs Cordage Company of San Francisco. He later became a California state senator. In 1880 he purchased 275 acres of Napa Valley land, planted a vineyard, and two years later built the winery.

A handsome mansion, Hillcrest, was built on top of a wooded hill—this was the Tubbs family country seat. (This beautiful landmark was burned to the ground in 1964.) Tubbs traveled to France, where he purchased cuttings from the most famous vineyards. He found much to admire in the architecture of their wineries, and when he returned home, using French stone masons and plans drawn by a French architect, the winery was constructed. Its facade is of imported cut stone; the rear and sides of native stone. It is, in the manner of that day, without steel reinforcing, its walls 42 inches thick at the rear, where it extends into the hillside—"built like a dam," says Lee Paschich, its present owner.

In 1886, Tubbs secured the services of French-born and trained Jerome Bardot as cellarmaster. He was a dedicated winemaker, and produced some outstanding vintages.

After the death of Alfred Tubbs in 1897, the winery was operated by his son William until 1919, when a grandson, Chapin F. Tubbs, took over the family holdings. Prohibition was the order of the day; vineyards were pulled out and orchards of pear and prune trees were planted. The winery fell into disuse for more than three decades.

In 1958, the estate was purchased by a Chinese couple, the Yort Franks. The Franks created a five-acre lake, with three islands crowned with red lacquer pavilions, curving bridges and an authentic Chinese junk. Weeping willows fringed the beautiful water gardens, and Frank re-named the estate, poetically, Jade Gardens. It was their family home until 1968, when it was sold to Lee Paschich.

In 1972 the new owner acquired two partners, James L. Barrett and Ernest W. Hahn, and reopened the winery. Chateau Montelena was furnished and equipped with modern winemaking equipment, and the services of a dedicated winemaker were enlisted—Miljenko (Mike) Grgich. Grgich is a Croatian-born enologist who received his training at the University of Zagreb in Jugoslavia. He came to the USA in 1958, worked for a time under American enologists at some of Napa Valley's most prestigious wineries.

Grgich is a conscientious winemaker with an enviable background, and believes firmly in the future of the valley and its wines. California winemaking has come of age, he says. "A new level of quality has been reached—there are more good grapes, better cooperage, more know-how. There are more experienced growers and winemakers, more appreciative wine drinkers, and of course more money."

Patchwork vegetation on the valley floor.

OTHER WINERIES

CONRADI VINEYARDS, at 3650 Spring Mountain Road, is owned by Art Martin. His winery is an old stone building, circa 1886, where he is engaged in making two wines, Cabernet Sauvignon and Zinfandel, which are scheduled for release in the near future. This winery started out in life as Martin's Spring Mountain Vineyards, but, owing to the similarity to the name of another winery, it was re-christened Conradi Vineyards.

J. MATHEWS WINERY, formerly known as Carbone Napa Valley Winery, is not a new venture, but recently changed hands after being in the Carbone family for many years. The winery, an old landmark built in 1882, is at the corner of Main and Young Sts., in downtown Napa. The new owner is Ken Nelson, who has moved the main winery operation to Newport Beach.

JUSTIN MILLER, 8329 Hwy. 29, does not have a winemaking operation, but has invented a process, known as Millerway Carbonation, for making "instant champagne." The process uses pressure to put the bubbles in, and the resulting bubbly wine has the advantage of producing tiny bubbles for a long time. He operates in a long building back of his home, where he has several processes available.

MOET-HENNESSY is a wholly owned subsidiary and holding company of a large French firm. Their mission is to provide this country with a fine Natural Champagne style sparkling wine, and they are going about it in a big way, with 800 acres of vineyard; 650 in Los Carneros, 170 on Mt. Veeder, and some 50 plantable acres at the winery site in Yountville.

It will be situated across from Vintage 1870 on Hwy. 29, on a knoll near the California Veterans Home. Plantings are Pinot Blanc, Folle Blance and Ugni Blanc. The Pinot Noir needed to produce their sparkling wine is purchased from Trefethen Vineyards. It will be made in the traditional Methode Champenois, and a staff from France will set up the winery, and make the wines.

NAPA VALLEY COOPERATIVE WINERY is a large, sprawling building south of the city of St. Helena. Their operation is exclusively that of making wine out of Napa Valley grapes for E. & J. Gallo, and sending it in tank trucks to Modesto. They have a large grower membership among valley viticulturists, and each grower is permitted to bottle enough of the resulting wine for his own use. The Co-op cellar is two wineries built together, the second around the first small old stone winery that had belonged to Oakland vintner Theodore Gier.

NASH CREEK VINEYARDS is the joint effort of Bob Key, Bill Stafford and Norm Sloane. Old stone cellars at 3520 Silverado Trail are being refurbished and the group will produce Zinfandel exclusively. Production will be 10,000 cases annually.

PICKLE CANYON VINEYARDS is the joint venture of John Wright, vineyard manager at Moet-Hennessy, and W. Herbert McGrew. These two ama-

A winter vineyard on White Sulpher Springs Lane.

teur enologists purchased a 76 acre parcel of land on Mt. Veeder, near the Moet-Hennessy holdings. They began the clearing and planting of the land in 1970; so far they have ten acres of Cabernet Sauvignon and Merlot. The wines will be bottled at a nearby winery.

RAYMOND VINEYARDS got under way in 1974, the winery of Roy Raymond and his two sons, members of the Beringer family. They continue to work at Beringer's as they construct and equip their own winery. They have planted a 90-acre vineyard adjacent to the winery site on Galleron Road, south of St. Helena.

SILVEROAKS CELLARS winery project is located at 915 Oakville Cross Road in Yountville. It was founded in 1972, the year of the first crush, and consists of crushing and aging facilities. Owners are Justin Meyer, formerly of Christian Brothers, who is the winemaker, and Roy Duncan of Denver. They will make Cabernet Sauvignon and other premium varietals not yet decided upon. The winery construction is planned for 1976 or 1977.

TREFETHEN VINEYARDS on Oak Knoll Road is owned by Gene Trefethen. Gene, with his son John and ranch manager Tony Baldini, have been in the business of custom farming for years. They came to Napa Valley to establish themselves in the grape growing business, acquired 600 acres of vines, extremely fine and beautifully cared for. Plantings include Pinot Noir, Chardonnay, White Riesling, Zinfandel and Merlot. They are at present crushing these grapes for Moet-Hennessy Vineyards, but when the latter's vines come into bearing, the Trefethens intend to make wine on their own.

VILLA MT. EDEN, on Oakville Cross Road near Silverado Trail is the property of James and Anne McWilliams, who have owned the ranch for five years. The old winery on the place is being readied for operation, and is part of a complex which includes a home and stables. It operated in the 1880's, under ownership of G.S. Meyers, using the Mt. Eden Vineyards label. The winemaker is Nils Venge, a graduate of the School of Enology and Viticulture, UC Davis. He received further training at Heitz Cellars and Charles Krug Winery. Pinot Noir, Gewurztraminer, Napa Gamay, Chardonnay, Cabernet Sauvignon and Chenin Blanc will be the wines. First crush was 1974.

WINERY LAKE features an old stone mansion resembling a castle on the Rhine, which was built by two French winemakers, Michael Debret and Pierre Priet, in the 1800's. It is the home of art collector and bon vivant Rene diRosa, who replanted the century-old vineyards to premium varieties. He plans, at a future date, to make wine there. When he does, he will build a new stone winery on the lake shore. However, he says he is having so much pleasure thinking about it that this may not happen for several more years.

CHARLIE WOODS has been constructing his winery for some time now. It is located on Highway 29 near Yountville. The owner is a designer and builder of the area, involved in the winery venture with his brother, W. R. Woods. The Woods brothers will make the wines themselves. These will include an estate bottled Chardonnay and a Cabernet Sauvignon. The first crush is scheduled for 1975. Production is visualized as 10,000 cases a year.

The aging caves at Schramsberg cellars.

APPENDIX

BEAULIEU VINEYARDS

Address: 1960 Highway 29, Rutherford
Phone: (707) 963-3671
Hours: 10 to 4 daily
Facilities: Tours, tasting, retail sales
Winemaker: Theo Rosenbrand
Wines: generic, varietal, dessert and sparkling wines
Vineyards: 745 acres
Volume: 1,800,000 gallons storage

BERINGER WINERY

Address: 2000 Main Street, St. Helena
Phone: (707) 963-7115
Hours: 9 to 4:45 daily
Facilities: Tasting, tours, sales gift shop
Winemaker: Myron Nightingale
Wines: varietal, generic, dessert, sparkling wines; brandy
Vineyards: 3,000 acres
Volume: 2.5 million gallons storage; 600,000 gallons fermenting; 200,000 cases per year

BURGESS CELLARS

Address: 1108 Deer Park Road, St. Helena
Phone: (707) 963-4766
Facilities: Sales, picnic area; informal tours; no tasting
Winemaker: Thomas Burgess
Wines: varietal and generic
Vineyards: 22 acres plus select purchased grapes
Volume: 2,000 cases per year, storage 37,000 gallons fermenting 9,000 gallons

CARNEROS CREEK WINERY

Address: 1285 Dealy Lane, Napa
Phone: (707) 226-3279
Hours: open by appointment
Facilities: tours; no tasting or sales
Winemaker: Francis Mahoney
Wines: Chardonnay, Cabernet, Pinot Noir, Zinfandel
Vineyards: 9 acres Pinot Noir plus select purchased grapes
Volume: 8700 gallons fermenting, 24,000 gallons storage

CAYMUS VINEYARDS

Address: 8700 Conn Creek Road, St. Helena
Phone: (707) 963-4204
Hours: by appointment, case sales only
Facilities: Tasting
Winemaker: Charles Wagner
Wines: Pinot Noir, Pinot Noir Blanc, Cabernet, Johannisberg Riesling
Vineyards: 70 acres
Volume: 20,000 gallons

CHAPPELLET VINEYARDS

Address: 1581 Sage Canyon Road, St. Helena
Phone: (707) 963-7136
Hours: by appointment only
Facilities: Group tours by appointment, sales by mailing list
Winemaker: Philip Togni
Wines: Chenin Blanc, Riesling, Chardonnay, Cabernet
Vineyards: 95 acres plus grapes from neighboring vineyards
Volume: 60,000 gallons storage

CHATEAU CHEVALIER
  Address: 3101 Spring Mountain Road, St. Helena
  Phone: (707) 963-2342
  Hours: by appointment only
  Facilities: Tours, advance appointment
  Winemaker: Greg Bissonette
  Wines: Cabernet, Chardonnay, Pinot Noir, White Riesling
  Vineyards: 60 acres plus purchased grapes
  Volume: 9,000 gallons fermenting, 15,000 gallons storage

CHATEAU MONTELENA
  Address: 1429 Tubbs Lane, Calistoga
  Phone: (707) 942-5105
  Hours: not open to public
  Facilities: group tours, appointment only
  Winemaker: Mike Grgich
  Wines: Chardonnay, Johannisberg Riesling, Cabernet, Zinfandel
  Vineyards: 100 acres plus purchased grapes
  Volume: 100,000 gallons storage

CHRISTIAN BROTHERS WINERY
  Address: 2555 North Main Street, St. Helena
  Phone: (707) 963-2719
  Hours: 10 to 4 daily
  Facilities: Tours, tasting, retail sales
  Winemaker: Brother Timothy
  Wines: varietal, generic, dessert champagne, vermouth, brandy
  Vineyards: 2,000 acres
  Volume: 20,000,000 gallons storage, 3,700,000 fermentation

CLOS DU VAL
  Address: 5584 Silverado Trail, Napa
  Phone: (707) 224-6387
  Hours: Production winery only
  Facilities: No public facilities
  Winemaker: Bernard Portet
  Wines: Cabernet Sauvignon, Zinfandel
  Vineyards: 120 acres
  Volume: 12,000-14,000 cases annually; storage, fermenting

CONRADI VINEYARDS
  Address: 3650 Spring Mountain Road, St. Helena
  Phone: (707) 963-7511
  Hours: not open to public
  Facilities: by appointment only
  Winemaker: Art Martin
  Wines: Cabernet Sauvignon, Zinfandel
  Vineyards: None
  Volume: 8,000 gallons storage

CUVAISON CELLARS
  Address: 4560 Silverado Trail North, Calistoga
  Phone: (707) 942-6100
  Hours: 10 to 4 daily
  Facilities: tasting, picnic tables
  Winemaker: Thomas Cottrell
  Wines: Varietals only
  Vineyards: 15 acres plus select purchased grapes
  Volume: 50,000 gallons; 18,000 cases

DIAMOND CREEK VINEYARDS
  Address: 1500 Diamond Mountain Road, Calistoga
  Phone: (415) 931-0293
  Hours: No visitor accomodations
  Facilities: Group tours and picnics by appointment only
  Winemaker: Alfred Brounstein
  Wines: 3 dictinct bottlings of Cabernet
  Vineyards: 20 acres
  Volume: 6,000 gallons

FRANCISCAN VINEYARDS
  Address: 1179 Galleron Road, St. Helena
  Phone: (707) 963-3886
  Hours: Open spring 1975
  Facilities: Tasting, tours, sales gift shop
  Winemaker: Leonard A. Berg
  Wines: dry table wines
  Vineyards: 250 acres plus purchased grapes
  Volume: 500,000 gallons

FREEMARK ABBEY WINERY
Addres: 3022 St. Helena Highway, St. Helena
Phone: (707) 963-7106
Hours: 11-4:30 for retail sales
Facilities: Tours, M-F 11 & 2; Weekends, 1:30 & 3
Winemaker: Jerry Luper
Wines: Cabernet Sauvignon, Pinot Noir, Chardonnay, Johannisberg Riesling
Vineyards: 200 acres
Volume: 20,000 cases annually

HEITZ WINE CELLARS
Address: 500 Taplin Road, St. Helena
Phone: (707) 963-3542
Hours: 11-4:30 at 436 Main Street
Facilities: tasting, retail sales
Winemaker: Joseph Heitz
Wines: Table, dessert and sparkling wines
Vineyards: 30 acres plus selected purchases
Volume: 85,000 gallons storage

INGLENOOK VINEYARDS
Address: Highway 29, Rutherford
Phone: (707) 963-7182
Hours: 9-5 daily
Facilities: Tasting, tours, sales gift shop
Winemaker: Thomas Farrell
Wines: generic, varietal, dessert and sparkling wines
Vineyards: 2800 acres in Napa Valley
Volume: 3,000 000 plus gallons fermentation

HANNS KORNELL CHAMPAGNE CELLARS
Address: 1091 Larkmead Lane, Calistoga
Phone: (707) 963-2334
Hours: 10 to 4:30 daily
Facilities: Tasting, tours, sales gift shop
Winemaker: Hanns Kornell
Vineyards: None
Volume: 30,000 cases

CHARLES KRUG WINERY
Address: Highway 29, St. Helena
Phone: (707) 963-2761
Hours: 10 to 4 daily
Facilities: Tours, tasting, retail sales
Winemaker: Peter Mondavi
Wines: varietal, generic, Chas. Krug label; varietal, generic, CK label
Vineyards: 12,000 acres
Volume: approx. 4 million gallons storage 230,000 gallons fermentation

LYNCREST VINEYARDS
Address: White Sulphur Springs Road, St. Helena
Phone: (707) 963-4736
Hours: not open to public
Facilities: none
Winemaker: John Henderson
Wines: Johannisberg Riesling, Chenin Blanc
Vineyards: 60 acres plus purchased grapes
Volume: 15,000 gallons storage

J. MATHEWS NAPA VALLEY WINERY
Address: 1711 Main Street, Napa
Phone: (707) 224-3222
Hours: 10 to 5 daily
Facilities: tasting, retail sales
Winemaker: not available
Wines: table, dessert wines, champagne
Vineyards: not available
Volume: 50,000 gallons storage

LOUIS MARTINI WINERY
Address: Highway 29, St. Helena
Phone: (707) 963-2736
Hours: 10 to 4 daily
Facilities: Tours, tasting, retail sales
Winemaker: Louis P. Martini
Wines: varietal, generic, dessert wines
Vineyards: 850 acres
Volume: 2,100,000 gallons storage, 100,000 gallons fermenting

MAYACAMAS VINEYARDS
Address: 1155 Lokoya Road, Napa
Phone: (707) 224-4030
Hours: by appointment only
Facilities: retail sales, tours
Winemaker: Bob Travers
Wines: Cabernet Sauvignon, Chardonnay, Late Harvest
   Zinfandel
Vineyards: 42 acres plus purchased grapes
Volume: 5,000 cases annually, 12,000 gallons fermenting

MOET-HENNESSY
Address: 1743 Mt. Veeder Road, Napa
Phone: (707) 224-2022
Hours: not open to public
Facilities: Construction begins 1975
Winemakers: Edmond Maudiere, Kim Giles
Wines: Sparkling wines only
Vineyards: 600 acres
Volume: undetermined

ROBERT MONDAVI WINERY
Address: 7801 Highway 29, Oakville
Phone: (707) 963-7156
Hours: 10:30 to 4 daily
Facilities: Tours, tasting, retail sales
Winemaker: Robert Mondavi
Wines: varietals, one dessert wine
Vineyards: 750 acres plus purchased grapes
Volume: 1,200,000 gallons storage 600,000 gallons
   fermenting

MT. VEEDER WINERY
Address: 1999 Mt. Veeder Road, Napa
Phone: (707) 224-4039
Hours: by appointment only
Facilities: tours, to be arranged
Winemaker: Kimbal Giles
Vineyards: 20 acres
Volume: 7,000 gallons fermenting 5,000 gallons annually

NASH CREEK VINEYARDS
Address: 3520 Silverado Trail,
Phone: No phone yet
Hours: Open by appointment
Facilities: None yet
Winemaker: Bob Key
Wines: Zinfandel only
Vineyards: 15 acres
Volume: 10,000 cases

NICHELINI VINEYARDS
Address: Highway 128, St. Helena
Phone (707) 963-3357
Hours: 10 to 4:30 daily
Facilities: Tasting, informal tours, sales picnicking
Winemaker: James Nichelini
Wines: varietals
Vineyards: 50 acres
Volume: 30,000 gallons storage

OAKVILLE VINEYARDS
Address: 7840 Highway 29, Oakville
Phone: (707) 944-2457
Hours: 10 to 4 daily
Facilities tasting; gift shop, sales, picnic area
Winemaker: Peter Becker
Wines: varietal, generic, sparkling wines
Vineyards: 300 acres
Volume: 750,000 gallons storage 155,000 gallons fer-
   menting

JOSEPH PHELPS VINEYARDS
Address: 200 Taplin Road, St. Helena
Phone: (707) 963-2745
Hours: by appointment after Dec. 1974
Facilities: tours, tasting, weekdays
Winemaker: Walter Schug
Wines: varietals
Vineyards: 100 acres plus purchased local grapes
Volume: 240,000 gallons storage 100,000 gallons fer-
   menting

POPE VALLEY WINERY
    Address: 6613 Pope Valley Road, St. Helena
    Phone: (707) 965-2192
    Hours: 10 to 4 weekends
    Facilities: tasting, tours, sales, picnic tables, hiking
    Winemaker: James Devitt
    Wines: varietals and generics
    Volume: 17,000 gallons storage 7,000 gallons fermenting

RAYMOND VINEYARDS
    Address: Galleron Road, St. Helena
    Phone: (707) 963-3141
    Hours: None available; under construction
    Facilities: None available; under construction
    Winemaker: Roy Raymond
    Wines: undetermined varietals
    Vineyards: 90 acres
    Volume: undetermined

SCHRAMSBERG VINEYARDS
    Address: Schramsberg Road, Calistoga
    Phone: (707) 942-4558
    Hours: by appointment only
    Facilities: Tours, retail sales
    Winemaker: Jack Davies
    Wines: Bottle fermented champagnes
    Vineyards: 50 acres
    Volume: 38,000 gallons fermentation   475,000 bottles
        aging 12,000 cases annually

SILVER OAKS CELLARS
    Address: 915 Oakville Crossroads, Yountville
    Phone: (707) 944-8170
    Hours: Not yet open to public
    Facilities: Not yet open to public
    Winemaker: Justin Meyer
    Wines: premium varietals
    Vineyards: not available
    Volume: undetermined

SOUVERAIN CELLARS
    Address: Souverain Road at Silverado Trail, Rutherford
    Phone: (707) 963-2759
    Hours: 8:30 to 4 daily
    Facilities: Tours 10 to 2:30; picnic area
    Winemaker: Philip Baxter
    Wines: varietals and generics
    Vineyards: None
    Volume: 220,000 gallons storage 75,000 gallons fer-
        menting

SPRING MOUNTAIN VINEYARDS
    Address: 2805 Spring Mountain Road, St. Helena
    Phone: (707) 963-4341
    Hours: by appointment only
    Facilities: none open to public
    Winemaker: Charles Ortman
    Wines: Varietals only
    Vineyards: 20 acres
    Volume: 15,000 cases

STAG'S LEAP WINE CELLARS
    Address: 5766 Silverado Trail, Napa
    Phone: (707) 255-4284
    Hours: Open by appointment only
    Facilities: None, except as above
    Winemaker: Warren Winiarski
    Wines: Varietal, Chenin Blanc, Petite Sirah
    Vineyards: 44 acres plus select purchased grapes
    Volume: 50,000 gallons

STAG'S LEAP WINERY
    Address: Stag's Leap Ranch, Yountville
    Phone: (707) 944-2792
    Hours: not open to public
    Facilities: sales by mailing list only
    Winemaker: Raul Dondel
    Wines: varietals
    Vineyards: 100 acres
    Volume: 50,000 gallons

STERLING VINEYARDS
Address: 1111 Dunaweal Lane, Calistoga
Phone: (707) 942-5151
Hours: 10:30 to 5 daily
Facilities: tasting, self-guided tours, sales
Winemaker: Ric Forman
Wines: varietals
Vineyards: 400 acres
Volume: 360,000 gallons storage 109,000 gallons fermenting

STONEGATE WINERY
Address: 1183 Dunaweal Lane, Calistoga
Phone: (707) 942-6500
Hours: not open to public
Facilities arranged by appointment
Winemaker: John Swetland
Wines: varietals
Vineyards: 17 acres plus managed vineyards
Volume: 42,000 gallons fermenting and storage 10,000 cases annually

STONY HILL VINEYARD
Address: 3331 North St. Helena Highway, St. Helena
Phone: (707) 963-2636
Hours: No regular hours
Facilities: visits arranged by written request
Winemaker: Fred McCrea
Wines: varietals
Vineyards: 30 acres
Volume: 7,000 gallons storage 8,700 gallons fermenting

SUTTER HOME WINERY
Address: 277 St. Helena Highway, St. Helena
Phone: (707) 963-3104
Hours: 9:30 to 5
Facilities: tasting, retail sales
Winemaker: Bob Trinchero
Wines: varietal, generic, dessert; specialize in Zinfandel
Vineyards: None
Volume: 50,000 gallons fermenting 20,000 gallons marketed annually

TREFETHEN VINEYARDS
Address: 1160 Oak Knoll Avenue, Napa
Phone: (707) 255-7703
Hours: Not yet in operation
Facilities: Not yet in operation
Winemaker: John Trefethen
Wines: None presently available
Vineyards: 600 acres
Volume: undetermined

VEEDERCREST VINEYARDS
Address: 2203 Mt. Veeder Road, Napa
Phone: (415) 849-3303
Hours: Not open yet
Facilities: Not open yet
Winemaker: A. W. Baxter
Wines: varietals
Vineyards: 135 acres
Volume: 2,000 gallons storage 1,000 gallons fermenting

VILLA MT. EDEN
Address: Mt. Eden Ranch, Oakville
Phone: (707) 944-2045
Hours: not open to public
Facilities: Available later
Winemaker: Nils Venge
Wines: varietals
Vineyards: not available
Volume: not available

YVERDON VINEYARDS
Address: 3728 Spring Mountain Road, St. Helena
Phone: (707) 963-3266
Hours: not open to public
Facilities: none available
Winemaker: Fred Aves
Wines: varietals
Vineyards: 110 acres
Volume: 50,000 gallons storage; 25,000 gallons fermenting

MICHAEL J. TOPOLOS is a native San Franciscan, who became interested in wine while in his teens, and later moved to the wine country to explore and intensify this interest. It has resulted in his becoming a wine buyer for a large shop, giving wine classes and lectures at colleges and universities, and workshops in many communities. He has written and lectured about wine for the past eight years. His latest venture is the reconditioning of an old vineyard and making his own wine. Mr. Topolos lives in a woodsy section of Glen Ellen, with his wife Gail and their assortment of friends—horses, dogs cats and geese.

BETTY DOPSON has been a resident of Napa Valley for the past 22 years, and has seen and written about the wine boom from its beginnings to its present apex of interest. She has written for many publications, among them the Oakland Tribune, San Francisco Examiner, Santa Rosa Press Democrat, and is currently associate editor of The Redwood Rancher, a magazine published in Santa Rosa. It is known for its Vintage Edition, devoted to wine and wineries. Mrs. Dopson lives with her husband Bill six miles from Calistoga on Mount St. Helena, in a redwood-and-stone house built with their own hands.

SEBASTIAN TITUS is a third generation Napa Valleyan, born there in 1940. He received his formal art education at San Francisco Art Institute, and since then has slowly developed his classical pen and ink style. Mr. Titus is internationally known, having had many museum and one-man showings in such diverse areas as New York, San Francisco and Santiago, Chile. He is well known for his pen and ink art winery calendars, but works in other media as well. He resides in Napa Valley with his wife Pilar and their two young children.

MICHAEL J. TOPOLOS   BETTY DOPSON   SEBASTIAN TITUS

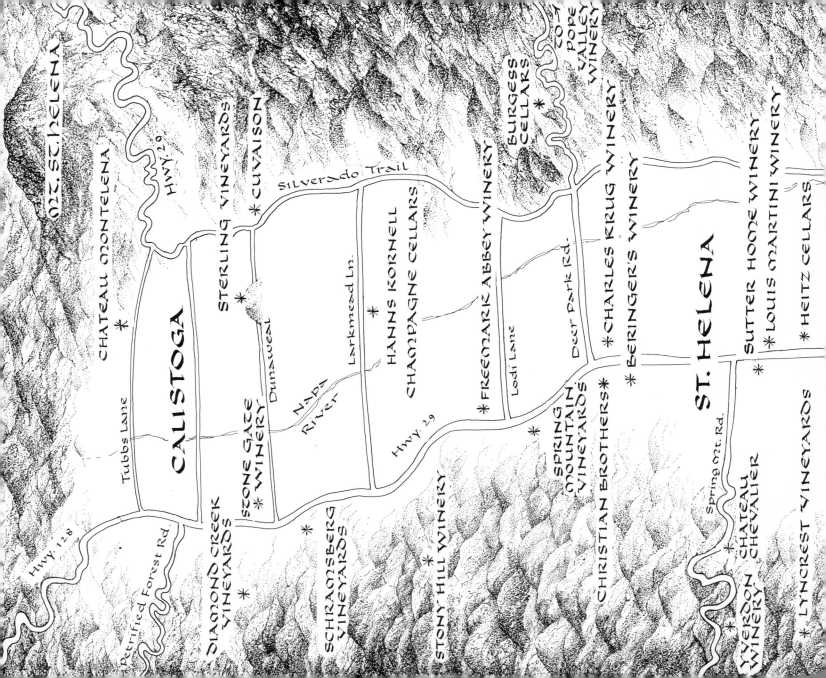

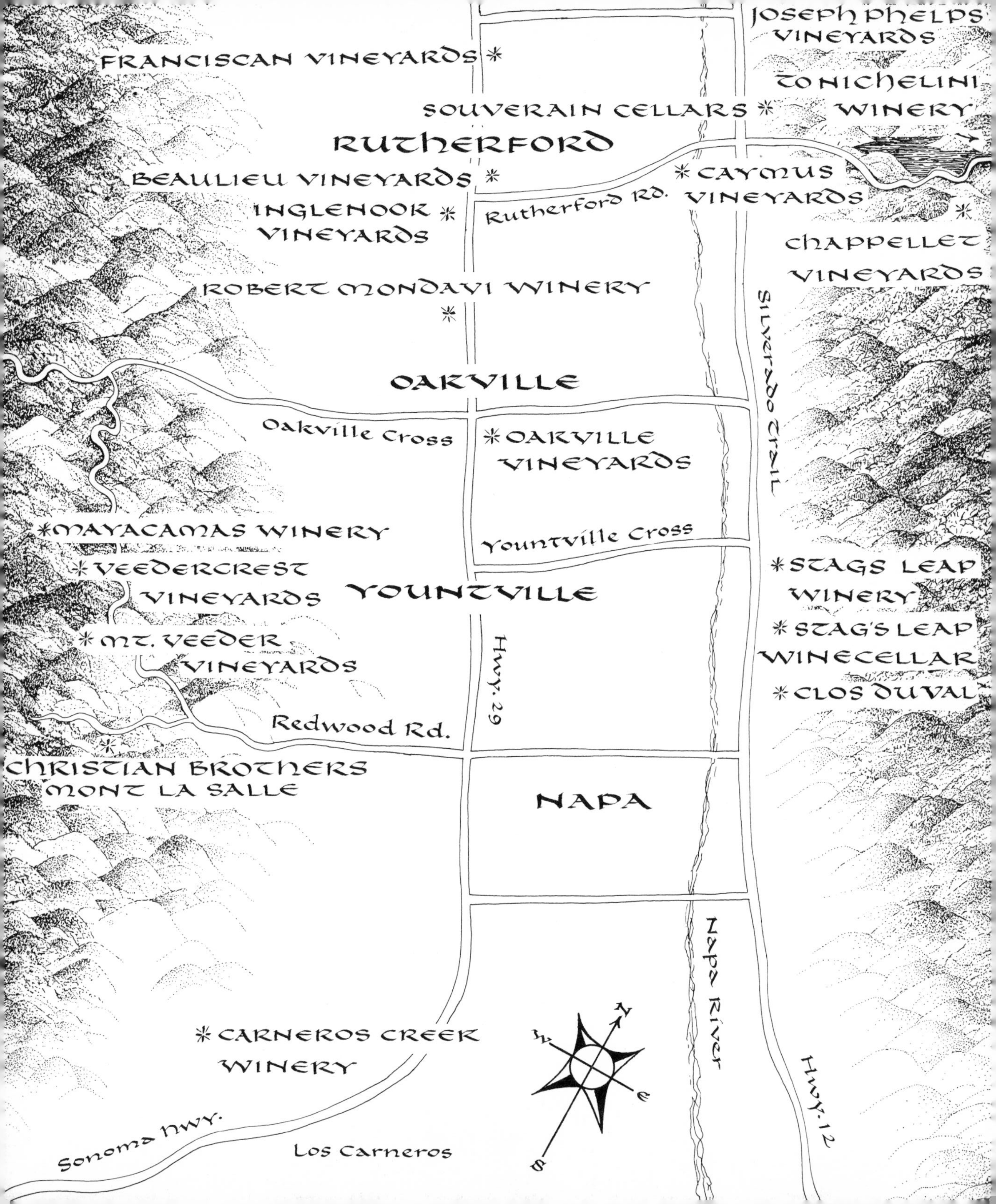

Joseph Phelps Vineyards

Tonichelini Winery

Caymus Vineyards

Chappellet Vineyards

Stags Leap Winery

Stags Leap Winecellar

Clos Duval

Hwy. 12

Silverado Trail

Napa River

Souverain Cellars

RUTHERFORD

Rutherford Rd.

ROBERT MONDAVI WINERY

OAKVILLE

OAKVILLE VINEYARDS

Yountville Cross

NAPA

N E W S

FRANCISCAN VINEYARDS

BEAULIEU VINEYARDS

INGLENOOK VINEYARDS

Oakville Cross

YOUNTVILLE

Hwy. 29

Redwood Rd.

MAYACAMAS WINERY

VEEDERCREST VINEYARDS

MT. VEEDER VINEYARDS

CHRISTIAN BROTHERS MONT LA SALLE

CARNEROS CREEK WINERY

Sonoma Hwy.

Los Carneros